CONTENTS

Ships in Focus Publications

Correspondence and editorial:
Roy Fenton
18 Durrington Avenue
London SW20 8NT
020 8879 3527
rfenton@rfenton.demon.co.uk

Orders and photographic:
John & Marion Clarkson
18 Franklands, Longton
Preston PR4 5PD
0845 0760078
shipsinfocus@btinternet.com
© 2007 Individual contributors,
John Clarkson and Roy Fenton.

Printed by Amadeus Press Ltd., Cleckheaton,
Yorkshire.
Designed by Hugh Smallwood, John Clarkson
and Roy Fenton.

SHIPS IN FOCUS RECORD
ISBN 1 901703 83 5

SUBSCRIPTION RATES FOR RECORD

Readers can start their subscription with any
issue, and are welcome to backdate it to
receive previous issues.

	3 issues	4 issues
UK	£24	£31
Europe (airmail)	£26	£34
Rest of the world (surface mail)	£26	£34
Rest of the world (airmail)	£31	£41

SHIPS IN FOCUS
July 20

CW00732455

No issue has been themed since 'Record' 3,
connections with Liverpool. The happy accident of having several submissions related to the Manchester Ship Canal decided us to do a similar job for that esteemed, but now altogether too quiet, waterway. We did not take much persuading, as one of us grew up almost alongside the Canal and both editors have spent many happy hours on its banks or near the entrance locks at Eastham. Choice of a 'Fleet in Focus' to feature was not difficult, as British and Continental vessels were a common sight on the Canal. Indeed, one of an editor's first photographs recorded the *Ardetta* and *Bittern* passing Stewart's Wharf, Ellesmere Port when sailing from Manchester for Flemish ports on a Friday evening in the spring of 1960. In order to present some images of the canal in its heyday, we have included 16 pages of colour in this issue, and we feel these nicely complement the black-and-white images from the negatives of C. Downs and others which feature in a selection from Nigel Farrell's superb collection.

Those who offered support for planned 'Fleet in Focus' features on Moss Hutchison and Prince Line post-war should not despair, as these will follow in due course once British and Continental concludes in 'Record' 38.

Although spring in the UK was early this year, the book we promised for spring is rather late. 'Clan Line: Illustrated Fleet History' is very far advanced, but printing will not be finished before August. The volume of work exceeded our expectations, but we believe it will be well worth the wait. The book is bigger than we originally envisaged, such is the wealth of photographs found, and the information included. To those who took up our pre-publication offer, the good news is that they have made a substantial saving on the publication price.

We are disturbed by reports of an outbreak of typographical errors in recent 'Records'. This is something we are at pains to avoid, each article being proof read at least three times by a combination of editors and authors, in addition to spell checking by computer. However, as authors readily acknowledge, picking up mistakes in an written piece that has become familiar is very difficult, so a new and strict regime has now been introduced whereby a third party gets to read everything. We do not fool ourselves into thinking that typos can be avoided, but we aim to keep them to a minimum.

John Clarkson   Roy Fenton

Rallus of the British and Continental Steamship Co. Ltd. in the Manchester Ship Canal. See 'Fleet in Focus'. *[Harry Stewart/J. and M. Clarkson]*

Among the numerous vessels of Cork Steamship which did not make it into British and Continental ownership because of the First World War was the *Dafila* built by Swan, Hunter and Wigham Richardson Ltd. in 1917. At 285 feet and 1,754gt, she was of the same size as *Jabiru* of 1911 (see page 7) but to a different design. On 21st July 1917 *Dafila* was torpedoed and sunk by the German submarine *U 45*, 85 miles off Fastnet whilst on a voyage from Valencia and Gibraltar to Liverpool with a cargo of iron ore and onions. *[Colin Turner collection]*

The *Jabiru* of 1911 fared better. She survived the war and passed in British and Continental ownership in 1922 and is seen here on the Manchester Ship Canal with her masts struck. *[Colin Turner collection]*

Fleet in Focus
BRITISH AND CONTINENTAL STEAM SHIP CO. LTD.
Part 1
Colin Turner and Roy Fenton

Although it was formed only in 1922, the British and Continental Steam Ship Co. Ltd. had a distinguished pedigree. Its origins lay over one hundred years earlier, with the St. Georges Steam Packet Company of 1821, which built up a network of steamer services on the Irish Sea. In 1843, under the influence of Ebenezer Pike, its centre of operations switched from Liverpool to Cork, with the title Cork Steamship Company adopted on financial reorganisation in 1844. Under the Pike family the company prospered. It split into two in 1871 when the Irish Sea services were transferred to a new company, the City of Cork Steam Packet Co. Ltd., the services to continental Europe continuing under the title Cork Steamship Co. Ltd. However, heavy losses during the First World War encouraged the Pike family to take up an offer in 1918 from the rapidly-expanding Coast Lines Ltd. for the City of Cork company and its services. Two years later a bid was accepted for the Cork Steamship Co. Ltd. from John Slater, head of Amalgamated Industrials Ltd., which controlled a variety of companies including the Heyn Line, the major Hull fishing fleet of Kelsall Brothers and Beeching, and a few coasters under Slater's own name. The fleet was rebuilt at considerable cost given the post-war demand for shipping, but Amalgamated Industrials was not financially sound and collapsed within two years. The Cork company was then acquired for £350,000 by a group of seven ship owners and agents (see table 1), most of whom had acted for the company and wanted to maintain their business.

Table 1: joint owners of the British and Continental Steam Ship Co. Ltd.

J.T. Fletcher and Co., Liverpool
Wilson, Son and Co., Liverpool
Clyde Shipping Co., Glasgow
George Heyn and Sons, Belfast
Phs. van Ommeren, Rotterdam
P.A. van Es, Rotterdam
John P. Best, Antwerp

To signify the change in ownership a new title was adopted, the British and Continental Steam Ship Co. Ltd., although use of bird names and the livery was continued unaltered apart from changes to the letters on the flag. Services were run from the UK to Amsterdam, Rotterdam, Terneuzen, Ghent, Antwerp, and Dunkirk. The company's main base was Queen's Dock, Liverpool but services also used Number 6 or Number 8 Dock, Manchester, and called at Glasgow, Belfast,

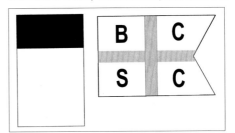

Company flag and funnel. The letters were blue with the cross in red.

A busy day at Number 6 Dock, Manchester in June 1935 with *Pandion* of 1926 (left) and *Serula* (right), bought in 1926, working cargo. The *Manchester Exporter* (5,277/1918) is further up the dock with Monroe's *Kyle Castle* (845/1919) alongside. At the far end of the dock is *The 250 Ton Crane*. [Ted Gray collection]

Egret (1) at Barrow-in-Furness with a Norwegian-owned Turret deck steamer ahead of her. *[Colin Turner collection]*

Barrow-in-Furness, Southampton and occasionally Ellesmere Port on the Manchester Ship Canal to load chemicals. General cargo was usually carried outward from the United Kingdom, with a variety of mainly bulk cargoes homeward: steel bars from Belgium to Ellesmere Port, silver sand for glassmaking from Antwerp to Liverpool, flax and cotton waste to Belfast. With so many ports the crew were kept busy: it was not unusual to enter ten different ports during a round trip of two weeks.

As the new company inherited an established network of services, there was little need for change, and the most apparent difference under the new ownership was that new ships were no longer routinely ordered from Swan, Hunter. Indeed, the *Tringa* was not even built in a British yard but in the Netherlands, reflecting the influence of the two Dutch owners.

Fluctuations in the numerical strength of the fleet occurred with changes in trade and through periodic losses.

The thirties saw trade shrink, and with it the older members of the fleet scrapped or sold foreign, with three going to one owner based in Sydney, Australia. Working in busy rivers and coastal waters, it is perhaps inevitable that a number of ships should have been lost due to collisions, beginning with the *Whimbrel* in 1926 and the *Fulmar* in 1927. These losses continued in post-war years, with the almost-new *Merganser* (2) in 1947 and the *Ousel* in 1957. In at least three of these cases the collision was due to negligence on the part of the other vessel. Geoff Holmes recalls sailing in the motor vessel *Egret* with a first officer who had been involved in three collisions in the Scheldt, and who always slept fully dressed when the ship was in that river.

The German occupation of the Netherlands, Belgium and France in 1940 effectively prevented the company trading, and the ships were redeployed, usually on British government service, although not before *Tringa* had been mined in the

Vanellus of 1922 with the *Ousel* (1922) and *Serula* (1918) in the Queens Dock, Liverpool. *[Colin Turner collection]*

Clangula, the last of three steamers from Cammell Laird, in the Manchester Ship Canal. *[Colin Turner collection]*

North Sea. Four further ships were lost through war causes, including two in the Mediterranean. War service also resulted in two ships being renamed, *Bittern* becoming *Imber* at the request of the Admiralty to avoid confusion with the sloop HMS *Bittern*, and *Nyroca* renamed *Sir Walter Venning* when she was converted to a cable ship. Unlike *Imber*, which remained thus until scrapped, *Nyroca* resumed her former name after the war.

It was largely the newer ships in the fleet which were sunk during the war, and so rebuilding was a priority, with three vessels being delivered in 1946. When the newest of these, *Merganser*, was lost after just eight months, the *Dundee* of 1934 was bought as a replacement. Renamed *Dotterel* it was found her speed of 16 knots was unnecessarily high and uneconomic, and she was operated on just two of her three boilers. As this suggests, the company was hardly innovative in its choice of machinery. Triple-expansion engines were being fitted as late as 1954, when the *Clangula* was delivered

as the last of three oil-fired steamers from Birkenhead. This ship brought the fleet up to its pre-war strength of 12, but almost immediately a cull of older ships was instituted, and in 1955 the fleet fell to just six. Only one further ship was delivered, the *Egret* of 1959, the company's first and only motor vessel. However, other vessels were chartered, usually owned by part of the Van Ommeren group.

The trading pattern for the *Egret* (3) in 1959 was to sail from the Mersey or Amsterdam on alternate Fridays and arrive at the other side on a Monday after a passage of just over 700 miles at a speed of 12.5 knots. Her running mates, the steamers *Ardetta* and *Bittern*, ran to Antwerp and Ghent and they too would make weekend passages. Through the English Channel the *Egret* would keep to the English coast, but sailings calling at French or Belgian ports would take the French side. The masters and first officers had pilotage certificates for the Mersey, although they needed a pilot and helmsman for the Manchester Ship Canal, and pilots at continental ports. It is interesting to contrast the *Egret*'s fortnightly schedule with a log of *Serula*'s movements in February and March 1935. She first made a return voyage from Liverpool and Barrow to Dunkirk and Antwerp and then one from Liverpool and Manchester to Dunkirk and Amsterdam. A round voyage in *Serula* took roughly four weeks.

The declining importance of trade between British west coast ports and continental Europe was hitting the company's business, and in 1961 there was no opposition to Phs. van Ommeren buying out the remaining shareholders, who mostly continued to operate as agents for the company in their home ports. As the remaining steamers were sold, chartered ships were used, but even this came to an end in July 1968, when the services were transferred to the Holland Stoomboot Maatschappij, who had been competitors for some years. *Egret* hung on a little longer thanks to a Manchester Prince Line charter, but her sale in 1972 brought to an end the ship owning activity of British and Continental, a history which could be traced back through its predecessor for just over 150 years.

Egret, British and Continental's only motorship, in Queens Dock on 29th September 1964. *[J. and M. Clarkson collection]*

The oldest ship taken over by British and Continental in 1922 was the *Avocet* of 1900. Broken up in 1932, her name was not repeated. *[Colin Turner collection]*

1. AVOCET 1922-1931

O.N. 109507 1,408g 688n
260.2 x 34.7 x 18.7 feet
T. 3-cyl. by Wigham Richardson and Co. Ltd., Newcastle-upon-Tyne; 199 NHP, 1,060 IHP, 10.75 knots.
15.9.1900: Launched by Wigham Richardson and Co. Ltd., Neptune Works, Walker, Newcastle-upon-Tyne (Yard No. 368).
10.1900: Registered in the ownership of the Cork Steamship Co. Ltd., Cork as AVOCET.
12.9.1922: Owners became the British and Continental Steamship Co. Ltd., Liverpool.
28.12.1931: Arrived at Port Glasgow and

broken up during 1932 by Smith and Co.
23.11.1932: Register closed.

2. HARELDA 1922-1938

O.N. 109510 1,288g 651n
255.0 x 33.7 x 18.6 feet
T. 3-cyl. by Wigham Richardson and Co. Ltd., Newcastle-upon-Tyne; 195 NHP, 1,060 IHP, 10.5 knots.
31.7.1901: Launched by Wigham Richardson and Co. Ltd., Neptune Works, Low Walker, Newcastle-upon-Tyne (Yard No. 379).
20.8.1901: Registered in the ownership of the Cork Steamship Co. Ltd., Cork as HARELDA.

2.1917: Requisitioned by the Admiralty, commissioned as a Q ship and operated as Q.34, ACTON, GANDY, HARELDA, and WOFFINGTON.
3.1919: Returned to owners.
13.9.1922: Owners became the British and Continental Steamship Co. Ltd., Liverpool.
5.11.1938: Sold to Bertram C. Hobbs, London.
19.11.1938: Sold to the Tai Yau Steamship Co. Ltd. (Mak Man Sang), Hong Kong and renamed HARALDAWINS.
10.12.1941: Torpedoed and sunk by the Japanese submarine I-124 eight miles off Barigayos Point, west of Luzon,

Harelda became a Second World War loss in the Pacific after her sale in 1938. *[Colin Turner collection]*

Egret (1). *[B. and A. Feilden/J. and M. Clarkson]*

Philippines whilst on a voyage from Hong Kong to Singapore.
5.1.1950: Register closed.

3. NYROCA (1) 1922-1931
O.N. 115115 1,295g 634n
255.4 x 33.8 x 18.6 feet
T. 3-cyl. by Wigham Richardson and Co. Ltd., Newcastle-upon-Tyne; 199 NHP, 1,060 IHP, 10.75 knots.
14.4.1903: Launched by Wigham Richardson and Co. Ltd., Neptune Works, Low Walker, Newcastle-upon-Tyne (Yard No. 401).
29.5.1903: Registered in the ownership of the Cork Steamship Co. Ltd., Cork as NYROCA.
1.1917: Requisition by the Admiralty, commissioned as a Q ship and operated as Q.26, MAVIS and NYROCA.
7.1918: Returned to owners.
21.9.1922: Owners became the British and Continental Steamship Co. Ltd., Liverpool.
12.1931: Sold to ship breakers.
15.6.1932: Arrived at Port Glasgow to be broken up.
19.7.1933: Register closed.

4. EGRET (1) 1922-1931
O.N. 115117 1,394g 691n
260 x 34.7 x 20.4 feet
T. 3-cyl. by Swan Hunter and Wigham Richardson Ltd., Newcastle-upon-Tyne; 199 NHP, 1,060 IHP, 10.75 knots.
23.9.1903: Launched by Swan Hunter and Wigham Richardson Ltd., Neptune Works, Low Walker, Newcastle-upon-Tyne (Yard No. 408).
22.10.1903: Registered in the ownership of the Cork Steamship Co. Ltd., Cork as EGRET.
12.9.1922: Owners became the British and Continental Steamship Co. Ltd., Liverpool.
1932: Broken up at Port Glasgow during fourth quarter.
19.7.1933: Register closed.

5. WHIMBREL 1922-1926
O.N. 120108 1,655g 848n
275.0 x 36.0 x 19.5 feet
T. 3-cyl. by Swan, Hunter and Wigham Richardson and Co. Ltd., Newcastle-upon-Tyne; 238 NHP, 1,300 IHP, 11 knots.

Whimbrel was British and Continental's first casualty, lost in collision in the Scheldt estuary in February 1926, although fortunately without loss of life. *[Roy Fenton collection]*

Jabiru. [Colin Turner collection]

20.3.1907: Launched by Swan, Hunter and Wigham Richardson and Co. Ltd., Neptune Works, Low Walker, Newcastle-upon-Tyne (Yard No. 788).
14.10.1907: Registered in the ownership of the Cork Steamship Co. Ltd., Cork as WHIMBREL.
11.1914: Requisition by the Admiralty and operated as an RFA store carrier.
5.1915: Returned to owners.
20.9.1922: Owners became the British and Continental Steamship Co. Ltd., Liverpool.
2.2.1926: Sank following a collision with the British steamer MARLOCH (10,667/1904) off Vlissingen in position 51.26.04 north by 03.34.02 east whilst on a voyage from Glasgow to Antwerp with general cargo. The crew of 23 were saved.
12.2.1926: Register closed.

6. JABIRU 1922-1933
O.N. 128306 1,703g 873n
285.0 x 36.1 x 19.5 feet
T. 3-cyl. by Swan, Hunter and Wigham Richardson and Co. Ltd., Newcastle-upon-Tyne; 254 NHP, 1,320 IHP, 11 knots.
10.10.1911: Launched by Swan, Hunter and Wigham Richardson and Co. Ltd., Neptune Works, Low Walker, Newcastle-upon-Tyne (Yard No. 866).
6.11.1911: Registered in the ownership of the Cork Steamship Co. Ltd., Cork as JABIRU.
12.1914: Requisitioned by the Admiralty as an RFA store carrier.
5.1916: Returned to owners.
12.9.1922: Owners became the British and Continental Steamship Co. Ltd., Liverpool.
1.11.1933: Register closed on sale to Scopinich & Monta, Genoa, Italy and renamed SABAUDIA.
1935: Sold to Capitaine Luigi Monta, Genoa.
1936: Sold to Dani & C., Genoa.
16.4.1941: Shelled and sunk by British

destroyers HMS JERVIS, HMS MOHAWK, HMS NUBIAN and HMS JANUS off Kerkennah Island, Tunisia in position 34.53 north by 09.50 east whilst on a voyage from Naples to Tripoli with a cargo of munitions.

7. IMBER (1) 1922-1934
O.N. 135716 2,154g 1,186n
300.0 x 40.0 x 20.9 feet
T. 3-cyl. by Swan, Hunter and Wigham Richardson and Co. Ltd., Newcastle-upon-Tyne; 370 NHP, 1,700 IHP, $12\frac{1}{2}$ knots.
10.2.1914: Launched by Swan, Hunter and Wigham Richardson and Co. Ltd., Neptune Works, Low Walker, Newcastle-upon-Tyne (Yard No. 926).
5.3.1914: Registered in the ownership of the Cork Steamship Co. Ltd., Cork as IMBER.
12.9.1922: Owners became the British and Continental Steamship Co. Ltd., Liverpool.
5.4.1934: Register closed on sale to Ingr. G. Angeloni, Genoa, Italy and renamed CITTA DI BERGAMO.
14.3.1943: Torpedoed and sunk by the British submarine HMS UNDAUNTED three miles east off Cape Spartivento, Calabria whilst on a voyage from Crotone to Messina. Refloated later that year and subsequently scrapped.

8. DOTTEREL (1) 1922-1929
O.N. 131372 1,740g 861n
260.0 x 36.0 x 22.2 feet
T. 3-cyl. by Barclay, Curle and Co. Ltd., Whiteinch, Glasgow; 152 NHP, 1,200 IHP, $10\frac{1}{2}$ knots.
28.7.1911: Launched by Barclay, Curle and Co. Ltd., Whiteinch, Glasgow (Yard No. 489).
23.8.1911: Registered in the ownership of Donald Currie and Co., London as POLAND.
20.3.1919: Sold to the Cork Steamship Co. Ltd., Cork.

24.4.1919: Renamed DOTTEREL.
20.9.1922: Owners became the British and Continental Steamship Co. Ltd., Liverpool.
8.1.1929: Register closed on sale to Compagnie Nationale Belge de Transport Maritimes (Armament Deppe, managers), Antwerp, Belgium and renamed BRABANT.
1934: Sold to the USSR, Leningard and renamed TOSNO.
1970: Deleted from Lloyd's Register for lack of up-to-date information.

9. CORMORANT 1922-1933
O.N. 137442 1,765g 862n
260.1 x 36.1 x 22.2 feet
T. 3-cyl. by Ramage and Ferguson Ltd., Leith; 152 NHP, 1,200 IHP, 12 knots.
14.1.1915: Launched by Ramage and Ferguson Ltd., Leith (Yard No. 240).
13.4.1915: Registered in the ownership of the Liverpool and Hamburg Steamship Co. Ltd. (Donald Currie and Co., managers), Liverpool as WESTMORELAND.
1.2.1919: Sold to the Cork Steamship Co. Ltd., Cork.
10.3.1919: Renamed CORMORANT.
12.9.1922: Owners became the British and Continental Steamship Co. Ltd., Liverpool.
25.3.1933: Register closed on sale to Societé Algéro Marocaine de Navigation, Casablanca, Morocco and renamed ORANAISE under the French flag.
1934: Managers became Scotto, Ambrossino Pugliese et Fils, Oran, Algeria.
13.8.1936: Capsized and sank opposite Bosquet Beach, 40 miles from Mostaganem whilst on a voyage from Mostaganem to Cette with a cargo of cereals, wine and passengers.

[To be concluded]

Top: *Imber* (1). *[Colin Turner collection]*

Middle: The first *Dotterel* was one of two near sisters bought by Cork Steamship in 1919. *[Colin Turner collection]*

Bottom: *Cormorant* on the Manchester Ship Canal. *[Colin Turner collection]*

SD14 UPDATE

Nigel Jones and David Hazell of The Shipping Information Servive (shipinform@aol.com) have kindly provided this summary of the current status of surviving SD14s and Prinasa 121s. The status of ships with names in italics is unknown. Note that Equasis change of flag dates are those when Equasis recorded the changes, not the dates of change.

Yard no.	Name per 'SD14'/'Record' 32	Flag	Year	Notes
875	*YUE YANG*	VCT	1972	
896	*TEPHYS*	CYP	1975	
904	*CANADIAN CHALLENGER*	BLZ	1976	Equasis 15.5.2006: Flag change to St. Kitts and Nevis.
906	JIN DA HAI	CHN	1976	Reported trading China.
1377	TANIA	GEO	1977	*2006:* To QSM Dubai Ltd., Panama; renamed QSM DUBAI.
1378	QING JIANG	CHN	1978	
1379	LUNDOGE	AGO	1979	Abandoned at Luanda Bay with a gaping hole in her hull.
1380	SONG DUONG	VNM	1979	*2006:* To Phuc Hai Shipping Co. Ltd., Vietnam; renamed PHUC HAI.
1381	PING JIANG	CHN	1978	
1383	AN YANG JIANG	CHN	1980	
1384	THAI BINH	VNM	1980	
1385	AN DONG JIANG	CHN	1979	
1387	EVER BRIGHT	PAN	1979	*2006:* To Pan East Shipping S.A., Panama; renamed EVER ACCESS. *2006:* To Korea Daesan Shipping Co., North Korea; renamed DAE SAN. *By 12.2006:* To Shantou Heping Sg. Co. Ltd., China; renamed HE PING 28.
1389	XI RUN	CHN	1979	
1390	STURDY FALCON	VNM	1980	
1391	PANGANI	SGP	1980	*2006:* To Tough Trader Maritime, Singapore; renamed TOUGH TRADER.
1394	SPRING		1979	Equasis 20.3.2006: Owner Masa Batam, Indonesia. Still laid up in 2007.
1395	DONG FANG 66	CHN	1979	Reported trading China.
1396	RYONG GANG 2	PRK	1980	Unconfirmed report of renaming DA TANG 82.
1397	NEW LEGEND STAR	HGK	1980	
1400	SAIGON 3	VNM	1980	
1401	SAIGON 5	VNM	1980	
1403	HUN JIANG	CHN	1981	
1414	YUAN JIANG	CHN	1981	
1415	FAR EAST	VNM	1982	
1417	CHANG PING	SGP	1982	
1418	HYANG RO BONG	PRK	1982	
1426	THEOFILOS [Note1]	PAN	1985	
419	*XIN HAI TENG*	CHN	1969	
428	SHU DE	CHN	1971	*2005:* To Cambodia and renamed WELLUCKY. *2007:* To Hongbo Shipping HK Co. Ltd., Cambodia; renamed HONG BO 3.
437	*HIE KHEAN*	HND	1973	
439	*HONG XIANG*	BLZ	1973	Equasis: flag unknown.
440	XIN HE ER HAO	CHN	1973	Reported trading China.
444	NIKOLAOS S	CYP	1974	*12.1999:* Broken up at Kolkata.
446	PAVONIS	VCT	1975	*26.3.2006:* Breaking up commenced at Chittagong.
448	NAVAL GENT	PAN	1975	*2006:* Renamed VALE (TUV flag). *6.4.2006:* Broken up at Alang.
452	*CANADIAN PIONEER*	PAN	1976	
458	*MONTE*	MLT	1977	
461	HERMES	THA	1977	*23.1.2007:* Beached Alang for breaking up.
462	DONG FA	CHN	1977	Reported trading China.
463	HAI JI SHUN	CHN	1978	Reported trading China.
464	NANKING	JOR	1978	
1349	ALDONA	PAN	1983	*About 1.10.2006:* Arrived Gadani Beach for breaking up.
1350	*WENG*	PAN	1983	
1357	PHUONG DONG 03	VNM	1986	
1358	PHUONG DONG 01	VNM	1986	
1359	PHUONG DONG 02	VNM	1986	
D569	JA GANG	PRK	1977	*3.3.2006:* Beached Chittagong for breaking up.
1063	*SAM HAI 1*	PRK	1970	Renaming SAM HAI 1 erroneous: last reported trading as KU RYONG.
1064	WANG JIANG	CHN	1970	*By 1.9.2004:* Renamed LI JIA (Chinese flag).
1073	SEA VENTURE	USA	1972	
1075	KUM GANG	PRK	1972	
47	ADREKNI	VCT	1978	Equasis 29.3.2005: Flag changed to Panama.
48	*EUN BONG*	PRK	1979	
51	PRESIDENTE RAMON S CASTILLO	ARG	1980	. Abandoned at Ibicuy, but unconfirmed report of sale to breakers.
92	*THETIS*	MLT	1974	
123	LISA L	MNG	1979	*2006:* Renamed TINA.
127	NONG GONG SHAN 8	CHN	1977	*By 28.9.2005:* Renamed JING REN (Chinese flag).
130	FORTUNE SEA	PAN	1979	
141	ORIENTAL KIKU	BHS	1983	*7.2003:* Renamed RONG NING 82 (Chinese flag). Trading China. Owners Xiang Shan Rongning Shipping Co. Ltd.
143	NAMA	PAN	1988	
145	GASPARD	PAN	1981	*2006:* To Sealink Shipping Corporation, Panama; renamed DALIA 1. *2006:* To Mahogany Maritime Ltd., Panama; renamed NORDANA.
147	SAFMARINE EVAGELIA	MLT	1981	*2005:* To Windsor Lines Ltd., Panama. *2006:* Renamed WINDSOR RUBY.
151	SAFMARINE MEROULA	CYP	1981	*2005:* To Windsor Lines Ltd, Panama. *2006:* Renamed WINDSOR LADY. *2007:* To Lily Shipping and Trading, Maldives; renamed LILY ROYAL.
152	JAIPUR	PRK	1981	Equasis 15.5.2006: Flag change to Jordan.
153	RA NAM	PRK	1982	
156	VEESHAM [Note 2]	PAN	1983	*2005:* To Shanghai Shipping (Group) Co., Panama; renamed SHANGHAI PRIDE.
157	SAFMARINE CONGO	CYP	1983	*2005:* To Windsor Lines Ltd, Panama. *2006:* Renamed WINDSOR STAR.
158	RYU GYONG	PRK	1983	
159	SAFMARINE NAMIBE	CYP	1983	Equasis 30.11.2004: Flag changed to Sri Lanka.
160	*FUDE*	VCT	1988	
99	*GOLDEN FUTURE*	PAN	1975	
132	LONG FU	PAN	1980	
134	*AMAR*	SGP	1980	*15.8.2006:* Reported on fire west of Nicobar Islands.
155	JAT NA MU	PRK	1982	*2006:* Renamed MAN PUNG.

Note 1: Refer 'Record' 32; reported sale to Indian breakers erroneous.

Note 2: Refer 'Record' 32; actually renamed VEESHAM not VEESHAM TRADER III.

FROM CANADA TO WALES: THE TALE OF AN MSC TUG
Captain Stephen Carter

In the years before the First World War towage on the St. Lawrence in Canada was dominated by one company, Sincennes and McNaughton Lines of Montreal. This company dates back to 1849 when Captain Felix Sincennes, who already owned tugs and barges, went into partnership with Montreal timber merchant William McNaughton. The business expanded and prospered, eventually owning a large fleet of tugs, and the company name was modernised to become the familiar SinMac. Being a well-established company, Sincennes and McNaughton tended to have new tugs built to their order, some in Canada and some in Europe, and this is the story of one of these tugs. Across the Atlantic in Barry and Cardiff, towage was undertaken by a variety of small companies each owning only a very few vessels, but by the 1950s - although various tugs were owned separately - towage operations were managed by the Guy family. Working away steadily was *Caroline Davies*, which was not quite the normal British tug design, but which nonetheless was a very useful member of the towage fleet for a number of years.

Canada
In 1909 the old-established Dumbarton shipbuilder Archibald McMillan and Sons completed two new steel tugs for Sincennes and McNaughton. The *Sin-Mac* was a fairly large seagoing tug, 138 feet long with a gross tonnage of 322, fitted with a triple-expansion steam engine. At the same time a smaller tug was completed. Named the *J.O. Gravel*, the latter was 94 feet long with a beam of 24 feet, her gross tonnage was 197 and she was powered by a two-cylinder compound engine of 54 NHP, 460 IHP. Following fitting out both tugs crossed the Atlantic and although they were recorded by the Canadian Minister of Marine and Fisheries in his annual report as having crossed under their own steam, it seems probable that, to save bunkers and manpower, the *Sin-Mac* towed the *J.O. Gravel*. Just who (or what) was the J.O. Gravel referred to has eluded researchers.

The *J.O. Gravel* was the archetypal North American/Canadian tug. A low wheelhouse stood in front of a long deck house at the after end of which was a large steam towing winch, and the deck house carried a single lifeboat stowed fore and aft on the midship line with two sets of radial davits, port and starboard, which would allow the boat to be launched from either side. A tall cowl-capped funnel with no rake gave the required draught for the coal-fired Scotch boiler. The tug's service with Sincennes and McNaughton was short for in 1913 she was purchased (it is thought after a short period of charter) by Roger Miller and Co. (PEI) Ltd. As far as can be ascertained, this company was a civil engineering contractor on Prince Edward Island, hence the PEI in the name. When the tug was purchased the company was engaged in building a new dock and landing at Borden, Prince Edward Island for a new Government rail ferry system. Part of this contract involved over 300,000 tons of rock being delivered by barge to the site and this is almost certainly what provided employment for the *J.O. Gravel*. This project was completed in 1916 and the tug was almost immediately purchased by the British War Office and renamed *HS 45*. Exactly what her war service comprised has not been established, but at some stage she re-crossed the Atlantic. Many sea-going tugs were used to tow barge loads of supplies across the English Channel to support the war effort in France, and the *HS 45* would seem to have been admirably suited to this work. In 1918 she was transferred to the British Admiralty and reverted to her original name, but whether the tug saw any use following the cessation of hostilities remains a mystery. What is known is that in 1920, following a period laid up awaiting sale, the *J.O. Gravel* was purchased by a firm of civil engineers, the General Works and Construction Company Ltd. of London, and renamed *Clarendon*. At the same time the company had two large sea-going dumb hopper barges, *GWC No 11* and *GWC No 12*, built by Lobnitz of Renfrew. These barges were 164 feet long with a beam of nearly 31 feet, had a gross tonnage of 460 and a carried some 830 tons of spoil to sea. They had donkey boilers which supplied steam to operate the anchor and mooring winches and, more importantly, the winches which opened and closed the hopper doors.

Manchester Ship Canal
The General Works and Construction Company Ltd. did not purchase these vessels on speculation. They had secured a contract for deepening the approach channel in the River Mersey to Eastham Locks on the Manchester Ship Canal, the spoil to be dumped at sea. This was preparatory work for the deepening of the Canal itself between Eastham and Stanlow in connection with a new oil terminal. In 1922 the ownership of the tug *Clarendon* and the two hoppers was transferred to S. Pearson and Sons (Contracting Department) Ltd., of London, but they continued working on

J.O. Gravel as built at Montreal in Sincennes and McNaughton ownership. *[Mac Mackay]*

The *Clarendon* at Eastham Locks on the Manchester Ship Canal in the ownership of either the General Works and Contstruction Co. Ltd. or S. Pearson and Sons. *[David Asprey]*

the deepening of the Ship Canal approach channel. Once again it is not clear from remaining records whether Pearsons, who at that time were well known as civil engineers for harbour works all over the world, took over the Manchester Ship Canal contract and purchased the three vessels, or took over or absorbed the General Works and Construction Company. Whatever the behind-the-scenes ownership arrangements, the *Clarendon* was used to tow the hoppers one at a time out to the dumping grounds off Hoylake, usually leaving Eastham on the last of the ebb, running with the tide out of the River Mersey and returning with the first of the flood tide. One change to the vessel made at some stage was the replacement of the large towing winch by a British-style towing hook, changing the towing method from a wire rope wound on to a drum to an ordinary rope which would have taken more handling by the crew. The hopper barges had some accommodation and a wheelhouse, and each hopper had its own crew who would open and close the doors, assist with the mooring, and steer the barge behind the tug when under tow. Their records indicate that the Manchester Ship Canal Company was paying Pearsons some £10,000 per year for the hire of the tug and two barges. In 1925, presumably after the completion of the

contract, Pearsons offered the three vessels for sale at auction, and the Ship Canal Company's ship brokers, C.W. Kellock and Co., were instructed to bid up to £20,000 for the trio. This bid was not accepted but following the auction Kellocks were able to secure the three craft for £21,000, the deal being struck on the 5th November 1925. Ship Canal Company records indicate that the vessels were purchased in preparation for the deepening of the Canal between Eastham and Stanlow as well as some works creating new berths at Ellesmere Port. The Canal Company insured the *Clarendon* for £6,000 and the barges for £9,500 each which, if this reflected the current values, showed that the purchase was at a favourable price. After purchase the barges were renamed *MSC Delta* and *MSC Gamma*, but the tug remained *Clarendon*.

When the deepening of the Canal commenced the *Clarendon* was again in regular use towing the barges one at a time to the dumping grounds off Hoylake, and she was remembered for the very loud and distinctive sound of her whistle as she steamed up and down the Mersey. The tug must have looked a little strange compared to the normal Mersey and Ship Canal tugs as she still retained her long North American-style deck house. On completion of the major dredging works the *Clarendon* spent long periods in lay up, but nonetheless was kept in good condition and occasionally emerged to tow the two barges to sea to dump. The tug and barges were certainly in use in 1933 when a new lay-by berth for the Lancashire Steel Company was constructed at Irlam. The contract to build the new facility was undertaken by Sir Alfred McAlpine and the spoil from the job was dumped at sea after being loaded into the barges by a large dragline crane.

Early in 1946 both the *Clarendon* and the two barges were taken on bare boat charter by the Westminster Dredging Co. Ltd., the tug being hired for £85 per week of seven days and the barges for £50 each for the same period. The charter was to last for six months with delivery being at Runcorn, and

One of the two sea-going dumb barges, *MSC Delta* or *MSC Gamma*, being loaded with spoil from the new Lancashire Steel berth at Irlam on the Manchester Ship Canal. *[Alan Hughes]*

Westminster had to operate and maintain the vessels and return them on completion of the charter in the same condition as when delivered. Included in the charter terms was a clause which required Westminster to insure the vessels, the *Clarendon* for £35,000 and the barges for £18,000 each. This gives an indication of the substantial increase in the value of shipping between the 1920s and the immediate post-Second War Period. Westminster Dredging probably hired this equipment on a fairly regular basis and certainly in 1949 were again hiring the two barges at £50 per week but this time not the tug, which appears to have been laid up for sale. In 1953 Westminster Dredging purchased the two barges for £28,000, and converted them to self-propulsion by fitting each with twin 300 BHP Paxman diesels driving twin screws. They became the *WD Delta* and *WD Gamma*.

South Wales

One might have thought that at this stage in her career the *Clarendon* would go to the breakers but, somewhat surprisingly, in 1952 the old tug was purchased for further service. In South Wales the family towage firm of J. Davies Towage and Salvage was looking for another tug and, although she was of unusual design for British tug owners, they purchased the *Clarendon* at what was probably just above her scrap value. Anecdotal evidence suggests that when a Davies crew went to pick up the tug the locals asked if they were taking her to be scrapped.

The *Clarendon* in the colours of the Manchester Ship Canal Company. *[Both: Ted Gray]*

The *Clarendon* steamed south to the Bristol Channel were she underwent something of a conversion. The after end of her long deck house was cut down and removed, and the towing hook moved much nearer amidships, British-style, and she was renamed *Caroline Davies* after a member of the

Davies family. At this time there were four towage companies operating in Cardiff and Barry: Edmund Hancock (1949) Ltd.; Bristol Channel Towage Ltd.; W.J. Guy and Sons; and J. Davies Towage and Salvage, each operating two tugs in their own livery. However, they were all managed as one fleet by Graham A. Guy of 53 James Street, Cardiff. At the two ports, tugs of the British Transport Commission usually (but not exclusively) did the towage within the dock, towing a ship to or from the locks, whilst the commercial tugs usually (but again not exclusively) towed the vessels to and from the seaward side of the locks. For most of her time at Cardiff and Barry the *Caroline Davies* was based at Barry and her master was Captain Horace Patterson. There the tug was regarded as quite a capable puller and she was always shown as being of 700 IHP. Now it will be remembered that when new the indicated horse power of the tug was listed as 480 and as far as can be ascertained she was never re-engined or re-boilered. However, one small note in the records of the Manchester Ship Canal Company

The *Caroline Davies* in South Wales soon after arrival and modifications. *[Paul Andow]*

13

may just give a clue. In a machinery and plant report on some overhaul repairs carried out to the tug *Clarendon* dated 7th September 1926 mention is made of work to the fan and engine of the forced draught to the boiler. Perhaps at some stage the boiler was altered to run at a higher pressure by the addition of forced draught equipment, a higher boiler pressure would increase the horsepower of the engine. During her time in South Wales an extra mast was added to enable a radio aerial to be rigged, the open top bridge was altered and the two large cowl ventilators removed. After a South Welsh career of just under 10 years, this much-travelled tug went to the breakers in 1962, when sold to Haulbowline Industries at Passage West, Cork.

Caroline Davies photographed in her final guise On the Bristol Channel by the late Desmond Harris (Fotoship).

Top: At Barry in 1956 after her cowl ventilators had been removed.

Middle: In September 1959 with the extra mast fitted to carry radio aerials and port side lifeboat removed.

Bottom: A stern view in July 1960.
[All: J. and M. Clarkson]

J. WHARTON (SHIPPING) LTD. Part 3
Ken Garrett

More new buildings

By 1978 it was recognised that the fleet, now composed of the ageing Goole-built quartet, was becoming outdated and the decision was made to modernise by building two new ships. They were to be the largest vessels ever managed by the company. Remaining loyal to local industry, the contract was given to Cochrane Shipbuilders Ltd. of Selby and the order was announced in January 1979. As before, it was a requirement that locally produced steel should be used in the construction. The ships were given the yard numbers 109 and 110 and were laid down in April of the same year. The first of the pair was launched as *Lizzonia* by Mrs Elizabeth Greetham on 5th December 1979 and the second as *Angelonia* by Mrs Fiona Wharton on 19th February 1980. To eyes more accustomed to the usual stern first launch when the ship gives a graceful curtsey once afloat and clear of the ways, a sideways launch can look quite spectacular. But things soon settle down and the expected tidal wave on the opposite bank rarely amounts to much. After fitting out, both vessels went down to Goole for dry-docking and final painting before running trials in the Humber and hand-over to the owners at Hull.

Although well equipped with modern electronic navigational aids, life rafts and rescue boat, the ships were otherwise traditional and not particularly innovative in design or outfit. The fixed four-bladed propeller was driven by a 735 kW eight-cylinder Mirrlees Blackstone oil engine through a reverse reduction gear box. All the crew were accommodated in single-berth cabins and the officers' saloon and crew mess room were located adjacent to the galley.

Single-pull Macgregor steel hatches covered the single hold that was divided, more or less in half, by a light transverse bulkhead at the mid length. In theory these bulkheads could be removed and landed ashore when not required, to be replaced and bolted back in position at a later stage. In practice they became the target for so many grabs and dump trucks that they were soon deformed to a point whereby removal and replacement became a costly and time consuming activity because of the fairing and repairs necessary to make them fit.

Both vessels were transferred to Everards in the 'demerger' that took place in July 1986 following a short period under Everard management after being taken over in the Thames. They performed well while in Wharton ownership although freight rates were very low when they entered service. They carried the normal run of coastal cargoes: coal, grain, china clay, road stone and fertilisers. The transverse bulkhead enabled them to carry two different grades of the same commodity without the problem of separation. In 1986 they were quickly integrated into their new owner's fleet and *Angelonia* was renamed *Comity* at Ipswich in June 1988 and *Lizzonia* was renamed *Capacity* at Milford Haven in February 1989. Both were sold in early 1994 to Onesimus Dorey (Shipping) Ltd. for demise charter to Torbulk Ltd. of Grimsby with Everards retaining the freight management.

Disposals

The four ships built at Goole were all sold between 1984 and 1986 and, while not strictly germane to this narrative, some of their later service has been quite interesting, in particular that of the larger pair, *Ecctonia* and *Gladonia*. The other pair were sold individually to the owner/master brothers Alan and Michael Whiting and although they had their moments they traded in the typical fashion of mature British coasters.

The *Gladonia* pursued a rake's progress after sale to owners in South Wales who obtained a provisional Honduran registration and renamed the vessel *Integrity*. She was loaded with second-hand motor vehicles and sailed for Georgetown, Guyana where the intention was to sell the ship after discharging the cargo. This plan was frustrated and eventually the ship returned to Barry in January 1986. She was laid up for a year before sale to Runwave Ltd. of Avonmouth. It then emerged that the British registration had not been cancelled and it was but a simple matter to quietly revert to the ship's original name and port of registry. Later, the registry was transferred to Gibraltar and then to St. Vincent and the Grenadines. If this was not confusing enough, she was then sold to a Spanish-based Egyptian owner in 1994. Following a couple of short voyages she loaded a cargo of rice in Rotterdam but was later detained in Setubal after damage to the cargo was discovered. Before all these problems occurred, she enjoyed a brief spell of stardom when, suitably disguised, she took the part of a pre-glasnost Russian ship and was filmed in Whitby for a television programme.

The *Ecctonia* was sold to Dennison Shipping of Kirkwall in Orkney and renamed *Vasa Sound*. With other Dennison ships she regularly took part in the sand trade from Loch Aline and, unfortunately, struck the Bogha Nuadh rocks. Contact with this hazard appeared to be a feature of the trade and the ship proceeded to Ipswich where she was declared a constructive total loss. After temporary repairs, she went on to Goole and was laid up while more repairs were carried out. She accumulated many debts and was eventually sold to a scrap merchant and sailed around to the Severn where, instead of being scrapped, she was slowly put through the outstanding surveys. Later as the *Sound* she was sold to owners in Hong Kong who intended to trade her between there and Indonesia with live fish as the *Sealion 5*. These plans were delayed when her

Lizzonia (2) in original pale blue livery. *[Charles Hill]*

15

main gearbox seized and a new unit had to be shipped out from the UK. The longevity of these ships says much for the robust building of the Goole shipyard and the careful maintenance bestowed on them by the company in their early years.

The final buildings

The associated company, F.T. Everard and Sons Ltd., had been considering a more modern type of dry cargo ship for some time. Specifications were sent to a number of British and foreign shipbuilders including some in the Far East. The replies from the latter were disappointing because, although they were keen and their price for a basic ship competitive, they were clearly unfamiliar with the degree of sophistication envisaged. European yards were unable to compete on time and price. Goole Shipbuilding produced a design but had difficulty in rising to the occasion. In the end it was Cochrane Shipbuilders of Selby who used the experience they had gained when building the *Norbrit Faith* (1,597/1983) and were able to project the ideas and develop an acceptable design.

Basically the ship was to have a box hold, strengthened for heavy cargoes with moveable bulkheads for separations and grain stability, an ergonomic bridge with generous electronic outfit and virtually all-round visibility. Lifesaving equipment comprised the recently introduced combination of inflatable life rafts and rescue boats. The engine room and machinery would need to be capable of being run and maintained by one engineer. The main engine would be able to propel the ship at a minimum of 10 knots on the smallest fuel consumption. A combination of controllable pitch propeller and a Schilling rudder envisaged a manoeuvrability that would obviate the need for tugs when berthing or unberthing. All these and many other labour saving features added together to provide a ship that could be run efficiently with a very small crew.

Above all, the ship was to have a cargo deadweight of 2,500 tons, be less than 800 gross tons and have a registered power of less than 750 kilowatts. These were the important break points in the contemporary British manning regulations. If exceeded, they would have meant carrying additional seafarers with higher qualifications, particularly if the ship was to venture beyond the immediate confines of UK coastal waters.

As things turned out, it was the availability of building berths and getting the keels laid before 18th June 1982 that became the crucial factor. After that date any new ship would have to be measured according to the 1969 International Tonnage Convention. Before that date ships could still be measured according to the British Tonnage Rules of 1967 with all the various paragraphs, imperfections and loopholes. As a result the keels of four ships, two each for Whartons and Everards, were laid on 15th June. Cochranes were able to lay three keels before the deadline and the fourth was laid by Richards Shipbuilders Ltd. of Lowestoft who built the ship from drawings supplied from Selby.

The ships were measured at 799 gross tons and this low figure materially helped their commercial performance for the first ten years of their lives by keeping port dues and other tonnage related costs to the absolute minimum. It was mandatory to remeasure the ships against the new regulations by July 1994 and the new gross tonnage was calculated at 1,892 tons. This 236% increase is a tribute to Cochrane's naval architects and a measure of how adept they had become in wringing the most from contemporary British regulations.

The first of the class, yard number 125, was launched by Mrs Brenda Blundell as *Willonia* on 23rd October 1983. After successful sea trials in the Humber the ship went to a lay-by berth in the Albert Dock at Hull for tests on the hatch covers and bulkheads. In order to give the maximum hatch opening and the minimum dead length of the hatch stowage area, the panels had been kept to four each side of the centre division with the inevitable result that they towered above the deck in the open position. The contract called for the Kvaerner hatch covers to be operated with the ship listed to 15 degrees and a three-foot trim either way. On board the effect was frightening and the master of a ship passing in the river during the tests was so alarmed that he informed the port authority that a ship was capsizing in the dock. But nothing untoward happened and after a few modifications the ship was accepted and sailed in early February.

The fourth ship of the group, yard number 127, was launched as *Stevonia* on 29th November 1985 by Mrs Gladys Wharton and was accepted by the company in March 1986. The initial application to name the ship *Brendonia* had been refused by the Registrar General for reasons mentioned earlier. *Willonia* had been managed by Everards since she was built and the agreement had been that this arrangement would continue until *Stevonia* entered service when the company would take over both its own ships. But by the time *Stevonia* came into service, the negotiations for the demerger of the company from Everards were at such an advanced stage that Everards assumed the management of the ship. They also continued to manage the *Willonia* although both ships retained the standard Wharton livery until after the demerger had been accomplished. The *Stevonia* was renamed *Sociality* while in dry dock at South Shields in February 1987 and *Willonia* was renamed *Sanguity* at Immingham in May 1988. Both ships remained on the Goole register.

At an average price of £2 million each they were not cheap but in service they came up to expectations and proved themselves to be versatile, operationally successful and as profitable as any comparable size ships during the difficult times they experienced.

Demerger

The demerger of the companies and Everards was probably the most significant corporate event since the original purchase of the shares by Everards in 1952. The nature of the transaction and the means by which it could be achieved had been the subject of detailed discussion for several years before it actually took place. It was an amicable affair and enabled both companies thereafter to pursue their own interests without reference to the other. As far as Steven Wharton was concerned, this meant being able to concentrate all his attention and resources on completing the development of Grove Wharf with the massive investment it required.

Once the formula had been agreed, the name of a dormant company, J. Wharton (Group) Ltd. (incorporated in 1982) was

Stevonia. [Charles Hill]

16

Stevonia (2) building at Selby. *[Ken Garrett]*

changed to F.T. Everard Shipping Ltd. of Gunness. On 26th June 1986, J. Wharton (Shipping) Ltd. sold the ships to the new company which also took their mortgages and liabilities and received a cash adjustment. The head office of F.T. Everard Shipping Ltd. was then transferred to Greenhithe in Kent.

The only remaining Trent Lighterage ship, *Ecctonia*, was on the market and was sold to Dennison Shipping Ltd. of Kirkwall who renamed her *Vasa Sound* after the sale docking at South Shields in November 1986. The Wharton group therefore ceased to be shipowners just five months short of the 50th anniversary of the first *Brendonia* coming into service in April 1937.

Postscript

Although the Wharton house flag and the 'Fleet that Jack built' were no longer to be seen around the coast, the operation at Gunness prospered. There were difficulties in the early 1990s with reduced tonnages and developments at Immingham whilst the re-opening of Hull Docks did not help but by being efficient, compact and operating under tight management control the company did better than survive and increased their tonnage. The spirit that drove the young Joseph Wharton to seek his livelihood at sea was still in evidence.

The late 1990s and early 2000s saw growth in cargo and the acquisition of land for the expansion of operations: first the adjacent Neap House Wharf and then a farm between the existing site and the village of Gunness. As such announcements must, it came as a shock when Steven Wharton made it known that he was selling the Grove Wharf business in a management buy-out. This was led by the company's general manager Martin Rees and the group accountant, Andrew Brown, both of whom had been with the company for a number of years. The new enterprise, Wharton Grove Wharf Ltd., commenced operations on 18th June 2005.

Steven Wharton thus became able to devote his time to Scunthorpe United Football Club and his farming interests which are somewhat more extensive than his grandfather's one acre and a single cow that started it all 130 years ago.

Notes on appearance

The original *Brendonia* appears to have had a dark grey hull and undoubtedly took this to her watery grave in 1939. Her small black funnel was embellished with a yellow band, red diamond and black letter W. During the war, the ships were painted in the standard Admiralty grey.

With the coming of peace the ships reverted to a company livery now slightly changed to a black hull, white superstructure, brown hatch coamings and masts. The wooden hatch boards were covered by black or dark grey tarpaulins. A white line followed the top of the main deck bulwark merging with the forecastle bulwark plating although there were individual variations. Sometimes the line would not carry on up the fashion plate to the forecastle head but continue the line of the main deck to the bow and, in one case at least, stopping short half way along.

The definitive Wharton livery can be said to have been reached with the *Gladonia* (2) of 1963 and her sisters where the ships' lines and colour scheme combined to produce a most handsome effect. The newly introduced steel hatch covers were painted green to add to the pleasing overall picture. All four ships had the same colour scheme and there were no differences between the J. Wharton (Shipping) and Trent Lighterage ships.

Over the years the funnel mark remained constant although the proportions were varied to suit particular funnels. In general terms the yellow band followed the line of the funnel top rather than the strictly horizontal band seen on many companies' funnels. There were variations on this simple theme and at least one ship had a horizontal band at one time while another had a band top slanting with the line of the funnel top and the lower edge parallel with the deck thus producing a wedge shape.

The *Trentonia* (1), a regular participant in the Channel Island produce trade, had the Huelin funnel mark for a while and when the new *Trentonia* (2) came into service in late 1964 she too had the Huelin mark.

The *Jack Wharton* always appeared in the bareboat charterer's livery of cream hull, white superstructure and cream funnel with the red and white diagonally quartered flag.

A new scheme was tried in 1980 with the building of *Lizzonia* (2) with a pale blue hull to complement the contemporary colours of the company's road vehicles, cranes and other shoreside plant. It was a short-lived experiment proving difficult and expensive to maintain and the ship and her sister quickly reverted to the more traditional black hull and white forecastle bulwarks. The scheme had reverted to the black hull when the *Willonia* entered service in 1984. For a short while later that year a narrow blue mourning band was painted around the ship as a mark of respect for Stan Smith, the late company secretary, who had worked for the company for over forty years.

Fleet list part 3

The list follows the usual Ships in Focus format, with the addition of port number and any relevant Commonwealth or foreign official numbers.

11. LIZZONIA (2) 1980-1986 1/1980 Goole.
O.N. 364574 798.06g 554.24n 1,315d
60.30 x 11.28 x 3.89 metres.
8-cyl 4SCSA oil engine made by Mirrlees Blackstone (Stockport) Ltd., Stockport, 222 x 292 mm; 735 kW, 11 knots
5.2.1980: Completed by Cochrane Shipbuilders Ltd., Selby (Yard No. 109) for J. Wharton (Shipping) Ltd., Gunness as LIZZONIA.
7.4.1986: Managers became F.T. Everard and Sons Management Ltd., Greenhithe.
30.6.1986: Owner became F.T. Everard Shipping Ltd., Greenhithe.
10.2.1989: Renamed CAPACITY.
17.1.1994: Sold to Onesimus Dorey (Shipowners) Ltd., Guernsey (Torbulk Ltd., Grimsby, managers) and renamed PENTLAND.
18.7.1994: Tonnages, ITC'69, became 909g, 518n, 1,315d.
1997: Registered in Bridgetown, Barbados. O.N. 725451.

This page, top; *Lizzonia*. [*Foto Flite, 21489*]

Middle: *Angelonia*. [*Foto Flite, 51942*]

Bottom: *Angelonia* approaching the Humber Bridge on 22nd July 1984. [*Roy Cressey*]

Opposite page top: *Willonia*. [*Foto Flite, 53702*]

Bottom: *Willonia* as the *Celtic Forester* at Goole on 20th April 2002. [*Roy Cressey*]

2000: Sold to Merlin Marine Ltd. (Torbulk Ltd., managers), Grimsby, renamed SEA KESTREL and registered in Barbados.
2003: Sold to Faversham Ships Ltd., Faversham, renamed ISLAY TRADER and registered in Barbados.
5.2005: Sold to Societa Co-operativa di Navigazione G. Guilietti a.r.l., Genoa, Italy, renamed SEA STAR and registered in Barbados.
6.2006: Sold to Auriga Shipping Co. Ltd., St Kitts and Nevis (Vita Marine SAM, Monaco)(Eurotec srl, Naples, managers).
8.2006: Still in service.

12. ANGELONIA 1980-1986 2/1980 Goole
O.N. 364575 798.06g 554.24n 1,315d
60.30 x 11.28 x 3.89 metres.
8-cyl 4SCSA oil engine made by Mirrlees Blackstone (Stockport) Ltd., Stockport, 222 x 292 mm; 735 kW, 11 knots.
2.4.1980: Completed by Cochrane Shipbuilders Ltd., Selby (Yard No. 110) for J. Wharton (Shipping) Ltd., Gunness as ANGELONIA.
14.4.1986: Managers became F.T. Everard and Sons Management Ltd., Greenhithe.
30.6.1980: Owner became F.T. Everard Shipping Ltd., Greenhithe.
1.6.1988: Renamed COMITY.
11.10.1993: Sold to Onesimus Dorey (Shipowners) Ltd., Guernsey (Torbulk Ltd., Grimsby, managers) and renamed PORTLAND.
18.7.1994: Tonnages, ITC'69, became 909g, 518n, 1,315d.
12.3.1997: Sold to John Fleming and Co. (Holdings) Ltd., Aberdeen (Hay and Co (Lerwick), Lerwick, managers).
17.6.1997: Renamed SHETLAND

TRADER and registered in Lerwick.
4.2002: Sold to Faversham Ships Ltd., Faversham.
6.2004: Registered in Bridgetown, Barbados
8.2006: Still in service.

13. WILLONIA 1984-1986 1/1984 Goole.
O.N. 364589 799.07g 585.45n 2,415d
79.00 x 12.68 x 4.55 metres.
6-cyl 4SCSA oil engine made by Krupp MaK. Maschinenbau G.m.b.H., Kiel, West Germany, 240 x 280 mm; 945 kW, 10 knots.
6.2.1984: Completed by Cochrane Shipbuilders Ltd., Selby (Yard No. 125) for J. Wharton (Shipping) Ltd., Gunness (F.T. Everard & Sons Management Ltd., Greenhithe, managers) as WILLONIA.
30.6.1986: Owners became F.T. Everard Shipping Ltd., Greenhithe.
6.5.1988: Renamed SANGUITY.
18.7.1994: Tonnages, ITC'69, became

1,892g, 1,044n, 2,887d and draft 5.10 metres.
5.2001: Sold to Charles M. Willie and Co (Shipping) Ltd., Cardiff, renamed CELTIC FORESTER and registered in Cardiff.
4.2006: Sold to Pisa Stevns Ltd., Antigua and Barbuda (THH Shipping ApS, Svendborg, Denmark) and renamed PIA STEVNS.
8.2006: Still in service.

14. STEVONIA (2) 1986 1/1986 Goole.
O.N. 364590 799.07g 585.45n 2,415d
79.00 x 12.68 x 4.55 metres.
6-cyl. 4SCSA oil engine made by Krupp MaK. Maschinenbau G.m.b.H., Kiel, West Germany; 240 x 280 mm, 945 kW, 10 knots.
6.3.1986: Completed by Cochrane Shipbuilders Ltd., Selby (Yard No. 127) for J. Wharton (Shipping) Ltd., Gunness (F.T. Everard and Sons management Ltd., Greenhithe, managers) as STEVONIA.

30.6.1986: Owner became F.T. Everard Shipping Ltd., Greenhithe.
9.2.1987: Renamed SOCIALITY.
18.7.1994: Tonnages, ITC'69, became 1,892g, 1,044n, 2,887d and draft 5.10 metres.
19.12.2000: Sold to Limarko UAB, Klaipeda, Lithuania and renamed SIUITA.
8.2006: Still in service.

Sailing vessel

S1. TRY ON 1888-1897 Two-masted wooden ketch 24/1867 Goole.
O.N. 58722 58.49g 43.02n
60.2 x 17.6 x 8.45 feet.
8.10.1867: Completed by Robert Stead, Wakefield for John Depledge (42/64 shares) and Samuel Depledge (22/64), Knottingley.
7.7.1881: Samuel Depledge, Knottingley became the sole owner.
21.1.1885: Mary Depledge, Knottingley became sole owner on the death of Samuel Depledge.
5.3.1885: Sold to Israel Jackson, Goole.
28.4.1885: Joseph Wharton appointed master at Goole.
5.4.1888: Owners became Israel Jackson (48/64), Goole, Joseph Wharton (16/64), Keadby.
22.4.1890: Joseph Wharton relieved by Harvey Woodward.
28.6.1897: Israel Jackson, Goole became sole owner.
5.10.1905: Hannah Jane Jackson, Goole became sole owner on the death of Israel Jackson.
31.5.1906: Sold to Charles Thompson, Hull. Registered 52/1906 in Hull.
2.11.1907: Sank in the Swin Middle Channel near the Gunfleet Beacon in the Thames Estuary while on passage from New Holland to London with a cargo of house coal. All crew saved.

Top: *Stevonia.* [Foto Flite, 46209]
Middle; *Stevonia* in the Thames with a crumpled bow. [J. and M. Clarkson collection]
Bottom: *Sociality* at Sunderland on 17th April 1999. [Roy Cressey]

20

ON BOARD THE FIRST SD14

In July 1984, the *Glasgow* discharged cattle feed in Birkenhead (below left, sailing). Dennis Cook and Bob Bowden made friends with the crew, and were invited on board. These are amongst the few internal photographs taken of an SD14, portraying the first to be delivered, as *Nicola*, in 1968. Dennis and Bob were taken with the friendliness of the Filipino crew and noted that, although she was in a poor external state (below right), her accommodation was spotless.

The chartroom.

The bridge.

The crew's messroom.

The chief cook in the galley.

Engine room telegraph and engine builder's plate.

The propellor shaft.

UP THE CANAL IN COLOUR

GREENPORT (above)
Permanente Metals Corporation, Yard No. 1, Richmond, California, USA, 1944; 7,097gt, 442 feet
Oil engine 2SCSA 6-cyl. by S.A. Fiat S.G.M., Turin, Italy; fitted 1950
Moored just inside the lock gates at Eastham is a Liberty with a difference, a motor ship. Built as the *Walter Wyman* in 1944, she spent a few months in the reserve fleet at Mobile post war, and in 1946 was sold to Italy, becoming *Italcielo*. In 1950 her owners had a Fiat diesel installed at Genoa, taking the opportunity to remodel her superstructure and funnel. She became *Greenport* in 1965, still in Italian ownership, although now under the Liberian flag,

with nominal owners Lloyd's Africa Ltd.

This photograph was taken on 26th March 1972 on what was practically her last voyage. After discharging her grain cargo in Manchester she spent some time laid up at Latchford, and was then sent for scrapping to Faslane, where Shipbreaking Industries Ltd. went to work on her. *[Paul Boot]*

EUCADIA (below)
Hawthorn, Leslie (Shipbuilders) Ltd., Newcastle-upon-Tyne, 1961; 5,924gt, 468 feet
Doxford-type oil engine 4SCSA 5-cyl. by Hawthorn, Leslie (Shipbuilders) Ltd., Newcastle-upon-Tyne

In 1965 Runcimans acquired a majority interest in the old-established Anchor Line. Instead of imposing their own colour scheme, the new owners adopted Anchor livery and in some cases its naming scheme for several of their own tramps, in this case *Linkmoor* which became *Eucadia* in 1968. Although not regular visitors to the Canal by the 1970s, Anchor were long-established traders to Manchester, as witness their *Circassia* in the accompanying feature of black-and-white photographs.

Photographed in July 1978, *Eucadia* was sold in 1981, and as *Sigirya* traded under the Sri Lankan flag until broken up at Gadani Beach in 1983. *[Nigel Bowker]*

WEATHER ADVISER

S.P. Austin and Co. Ltd.,
Sunderland, 1943,
1,405gt, 252 feet
T. 4-cyl. by George Clark Ltd.,
Sunderland

A decidedly unusual visitor to the Ship Canal was this ocean weather ship, arriving for dry docking on 1st July 1976. She had been converted from the Castle-class corvette HMS *Amberley Castle* at Blyth in 1960, and was going to Manchester for rebuilding from which she emerged as *Admiral Fitzroy*. She was broken up at Troon early in 1982. *[Nigel Bowker]*

NEMEO

R. and W. Hawthorn Leslie and
Co. Ltd., Hebburn, 1954;
11,018gt, 547 feet
Doxford-type oil engine 2SCSA 6-
cyl. by R. and W. Hawthorn Leslie
and Co. Ltd., Hebburn

Opened in 1953, the Queen Elizabeth II Oil Dock at Eastham was built once the tankers ordered after the Second World War had grown too big to navigate the Ship Canal to Shell's refinery at Stanlow. One of the editors remembers, as a small child, being taken to see the excavations and, gazing from the point where Paul Boot later stood to take this photograph, being awestruck by the depth of the workings.

Construction of an enclosed dock showed a singular lack of foresight, as – of surprise only to Ship Canal planners – tankers continued to grow in size, so that the dock was soon incapable of accommodating the current crude carriers. The answer was the Tranmere Oil Terminal further down the Mersey, and later an offshore installation in Anglesey. The dock did enjoy a second career, however, as products tankers grew in size. In the sixties and seventies, it was not unusual to see at least three berths filled. The dock still sees some use.

Photographed on 26th March 1972, the Liberian flag

Nemeo was an occasional visitor, perhaps more familiar as *Border Fusilier* of the Lowland Tanker Co. Ltd. – the distinctive tripod signal mast is a giveaway. *Nemeo's* owners were probably Greek, but their agents were the Southern Shipping and Finance Co. Ltd. of London. They were unusual in giving each of their tankers an individualised funnel marking comprising an anchor device with the initial letters of the single-ship company that owned it. In *Nemeo's* case these were N S for the Nemeo Shipping Corporation. She was broken up at Gadani Beach in 1975. *[Paul Boot]*

AULICA (above)
Kieler Howaldtswerke A.G., Kiel, West Germany, 1960; 12,321gt, 560 feet
Steam turbines by Howaldtswerke Hamburg A.G., Hamburg, West Germany
No photographic feature on the Manchester Ship Canal in the sixties and seventies would be complete without one of the Shell tankers which came in on almost every tide (and where are they now?). Passing Ellesmere Port's lengthy quay whilst outward bound from Stanlow on 11th May 1974 is *Aulica*, one of a large batch of 12,000-tonners with 'streamlined' superstructure. For a tanker, *Aulica* had a respectably long life: she arrived at Gadani Beach for demolition in December 1984. *[Roy Fenton]*

TABOR (right)
Caledon Shipbuilding and Engineering Co. Ltd., Dundee, 1952; 3,694gt, 385 feet
Doxford-type oil engine 2SCSA 4-cyl. by Hawthorn, Leslie and Co. Ltd., Hebburn
Ellesmere Port had the distinct advantage that ships could reach it without lowering their masts and removing their funnel tops, and at various times the port has been relatively busy. In the 1960s one of the editors regularly cycled past on his way to school, and could usually count three or four ships on the berths. Moss Hutchison's *Tabor* was photographed there on 23rd October 1974. Happily, the only sign of parent P&O's penchant for imposing corporate identity was the flying of their house flag: her funnel and the rest of her livery has remained unchanged.

      Tabor was sold in 1975, to become *Katia*, a name which was amended to *Kate* in 1982, shortly before she was broken up at Beypore. *[Roy Fenton]*

CEOL MOR (above)
Scheepswerf 'Friesland' N.V., Lemmer, Netherlands, 1960; 394gt, 159 feet
Oil engine 4SCSA 4-cyl. by Appingedammer Brons, Appingedam, Netherlands
As Craig Carter explains elsewhere in this issue, much of the spoil from dredging the Ship Canal was sent ashore at Frodsham, and a barge-full can be seen arriving there in the foreground of this photograph. Passing on 3rd November 1981 is one of numerous Dutch coasters which gravitated to the British flag in the sixties and seventies. They were usually owned by single-ship companies, in *Ceol Mor's* case the rather frivolously-named Jigwain Ltd. Her original name was *Lingeborg* and until 1978 she had been *Favel*. *Ceol Mor* lost her name in 1984 when she became *Lady Lotmore*, and then became the unpronounceable *Lady L'Belle* in 1996, as which she was owned in Equatorial Guinea. She had an undignified end: sinking at her moorings at Puerto Cabello, Venezuela in October 2004 after she had been abandoned following arrest for drug smuggling.
[Reg Bailey]

MANCHESTER CITY (above)
Blythswood Shipbuilding Co. Ltd., Glasgow, 1937; 5,600g, 431 feet
Steam turbines by David Rowan and Co. Ltd., Glasgow
Manchester City wears what was for her an unusual livery: light green hull with dark green boot topping. It is said this colour was adopted in place of the traditional black so that the hulls became less hot in summer passages from Chicago where lard was frequently loaded. Whilst it might have suited the newer ships, this livery seemed somewhat undignified on the pre-war survivors. Photographed passing Runcorn, *Manchester City* was broken up at Faslane in 1964.
[Eddie Jackson]

PACIFIC ENVOY (above)
Vickers-Armstrongs Ltd.,
Newcastle-upon-Tyne, 1958;
9,439gt, 501 feet
Geared steam turbines by Parsons
Marine Steam Turbine Co. Ltd.,
Wallsend-on-Tyne
Familiar visitors to the Ship Canal
were the Furness North Pacific ships
operating a service to Vancouver
which began almost as soon as the
Panama Canal opened in 1914 (see
'Record' 14 and 15). This shot of
Pacific Envoy in the late 1950s is of
particular interest in showing the
Runcorn to Widnes road bridge under
construction. Note the two derricks
perched precariously at the ends of

the incomplete arch, and the
temporary stays and A frames to
support the cantilevered sections of
the steelwork. The transporter bridge
which it replaced can be seen in the
background, along with the even older
rail bridge.

Pacific Envoy had a larger
refrigerator capacity than its forebears,
and this contributed to her 1967
transfer to Royal Mail routes as *Loch
Ryan*. Sold in 1970 she became
Aegis Strength until broken up at
Whampoa in 1974. *[Eddie Jackson]*

MSC ARCHER (below)
Henry Robb Ltd., Leith, 1938;
144gt, 92 feet

C. 2-cyl. by Aitchison, Blair Ltd.,
Clydebank
The star of this April 1963 photograph
is the steam tug assisting another of
Furness's regular traders, *Pacific
Reliance* (9,442/1951), a near sister to
Pacific Envoy (but note the funnel top
and difference in masts). *MSC Archer*
looks venerable, but was built as
recently (in tug terms) as 1938. She
lasted in Manchester Ship Canal
ownership until 1967. Sold to Maltese
owners in 1970, it is likely that they
intended to fit her with a diesel engine,
but there is no record of her fate, and
she was probably broken up in Malta.
[Eddie Jackson]

BLACK PRINCE (upper)
*Burntisland Shipbuilding Co.
Ltd., Burntisland, 1955; 3,597gt,
372 feet
Oil engine 2SCSA 4-cyl. by Hawthorn
Leslie (Engineering). Ltd., Hebburn*

Prince Line's smaller cargo ships had a regular service from Manchester to the Mediterranean, run in partnership with their fellow member of the Furness Group, Manchester Liners. The fourth of the name, *Black Prince*

was sold in 1971 to become *Maria B*, as which she was abandoned by her crew off the west coast of Africa following an engine room fire in March 1977. [Eddie Jackson]

ONDO (lower)
*Harland and Wolff Ltd., Belfast, 1956;
5,435g, 450 feet
Burmeister & Wain-type oil
engine 2SCSA 4-cyl. by Harland
and Wolff Ltd., Belfast*
In the 1950s Elder, Dempster built a class of five ships, two of which did not have passenger accommodation, the *Oti* and the *Ondo*, the latter seen

passing Old Quay, Runcorn assisted by *MSC Firefly*. This colour photograph may be unique, as *Ondo* was an unfortunate and short-lived ship. On 6th December 1961 she was heading for the Kiel Canal to complete her voyage from Sapele to Riga. A gale estimated at Force 10 was blowing, and the pilot boat approaching the *Ondo* capsized.

The *Ondo's* engines were stopped to avoid danger to the men in the water, and she was blown on to a sandbank. Her remains are still there, despite at least three salvage attempts. Her sacrifice was in vain as, tragically, the entire crew of the pilot vessel was lost. [Eddie Jackson]

THE LADY GWENDOLEN (above)
*Ardrossan Dockyard Co. Ltd.,
Ardrossan, 1953; 1,164gt, 205 feet
Oil engine 2SCSA 6-cyl. by British
Polar Engines Ltd., Glasgow*
Aficionados of stout maintained that Guinness was better in the north of England than in the south because supplies came direct from the St. James Gate Brewery in Dublin to Liverpool and Manchester. It was brought in tanks dropped into the holds of relatively conventional coasters. Less conventional was their smart, deep-blue hull colour, apparent in Eddie Jackson's fine photograph of *The Lady Gwendolen* passing Runcorn. She was replaced in 1976, becoming *Paros,* only to be sunk in collision in Ravenna Roads in November 1979. *[Eddie Jackson]*

MIRANDA GUINNESS (below)
*Charles Hill and Sons Ltd.,
Bristol; 1976; 1,451gt, 71 metres
Two oil engines 4SCSA 12-cyl. by
British Polar Engines Ltd., Glasgow*

Replacement for *The Lady Gwendolen* was *Miranda Guinness*, a purpose-built beer tanker, and also the last product of the Albion Dockyard at Bristol. She is seen passing Old Quay Workshops, Runcorn, on 17th June 1984, having discharged her cargo at Runcorn. With the decision to ship Guinness concentrate across the Irish Sea in conventional liquid containers, *Miranda Guinness* became redundant in 1994 and was scrapped on the Mersey at the tender age of 18. *[Reg Bailey]*

AMERICAN VETERAN (above)
Moore Dry Dock Company, Oakland, California, USA, 1945, 8,279gt, 460 feet
Two steam turbines by General Electric Company, Lynn, Massachusetts, USA
The effect of removing tall funnels and masts can be readily seen as this C2-type passes Old Quay. United States Lines had regular sailings to Manchester, yet for every voyage up the Canal their ships had to leave their funnels behind at Eastham. *American Veteran* had been built for the United States Maritime Commission as *Wild Wave*, a name chosen to commemorate the romantically-named US softwood clippers, given that the C2s were relatively fast, turbine-engined ships. She carried the name *American Veteran* from 1946 until 1968 when she became the *Trans-Oceanic Explorer*. She was broken up at Kaohsiung in 1970. *[Eddie Jackson]*

BRUSE JARL (below)
Kockums M/V, Malmo, Sweden; 1943; 8,428gt, 496 feet
MAN-type oil engine 2SCDA 7-cyl. by Kockums M/V, Malmo, Sweden
Looking immaculate, with her light hull contrasting with a threatening sky, the Norwegian tanker *Bruse Jarl* waits at Runcorn whilst an inward-bound ship passes under the bridges. Her fine looks belie the fact that she was a war baby, completed in Sweden as *Lillöhus* right in the middle of the Second World War. This was something of an act of faith by Swedish builders and owners, as she could not have left the Baltic at the time, and in that sea there was little employment for tankers. In 1956 she was acquired by Det Nordenfjeldske D/S of Trondheim and given the name *Bruse Jarl*. She was broken up in Spain in 1962. *[Eddie Jackson]*

GEORGE (above)
*William Doxford and Sons Ltd.,
Sunderland, 1954; 8,366gt, 464 feet
Oil engine 4SCSA 4-cyl. by William
Doxford and Sons Ltd., Sunderland*
Barrister had just been renamed
George in Manchester and had the red
band on her Harrison Line funnel
painted out when photographed near
Ince on 29th September 1974. Her
holds had been partly flooded to bring
her air draft down to the regulation 70
feet, and – now clear of any bridges –
her heavy-lift derrick has been raised.

In 1976 she underwent a mild
renaming to *Georgy*, but was laid up at
Piraeus shortly afterwards. She was
not broken up until 1984 when she
was demolished at Castellon. [*Paul
Boot*]

IRIS (below)
*Cammell Laird and Co. (Shipbuilders
and Engineers) Ltd., Birkenhead,
1954; 6,042gt, 470 feet
Oil engine 2SCSA 6-cyl. by Sulzer
Brothers Ltd., Winterthur, Switzerland*

A peculiarity of the Manchester Ship
Canal is that vessels can appear to be
sailing through green fields. Here *Iris*
passes Moore Lane Swing Bridge on
31st August 1980 during one of her
voyages to South Africa carrying soda
ash which she loaded at the former
coal tips at Partington. The Greek
tramp had local connections, having
been built at Birkenhead as *Doris*, as
which she ran until 1973. She lost the
name *Iris* in 1981, becoming *Kastro K*
and later *Stepon*, and was demolished
in Pakistan during 1984. [*Paul Boot*]

PHOTINIA (above)

John Readhead and Sons Ltd., South Shields, 1961; 7,676gt, 480 feet
Doxford-type 2SCSA 4-cyl. oil engine by North Eastern Marine Engineering Co. Ltd., Wallsend

In Number 8 Dock on 18th November 1975 is Stag Line's bulker *Photinia*, which had the distinction of being built in South Shields and owned just across the river in North Shields. After working as a cable layer between 1962 and 1965, she was reconverted to a cargo ship. Her end came in one of the violent storms which can hit the Great Lakes. On 12th May 1978 she was awaiting a berth at Milwaukee when driven aground after dragging her anchors. She was quickly declared a

constructive total loss, and after refloating was broken up locally.

Beyond *Photinia* are the Dutch coaster *Andairon* (458/1961), which was running on the Anglo-Iberian service to Spain, and the *Eucadia*. *[Nigel Bowker]*

KINGSNORTH FISHER (below)

Hall, Russell and Co. Ltd., Aberdeen, 1966; 2,355gt, 285 feet
Two oil engines 4SCSA 6-cyl. by W.H. Allen, Sons and Co. Ltd., Bedford

One of the last regular users of the Pomona Docks, at the inland end of the Manchester system, were two heavy-lift ships built especially to carry large items of electrical equipment to UK power stations. *Kingsnorth Fisher* was

operated by James Fisher and Sons Ltd. of Barrow-in-Furness but, as the large letter on her bridge front signifies, was on long-term charter to the once-state-owned electricity industry. The two ships actually used the roll-on, roll-off concept; low-loaders carrying the kit were driven on and the trailer and its load lowered into the hold. On board *Kingsnorth Fisher* on 4th May 1970 can be seen one of the tractors which will have hauled the load, almost certainly from the nearby Trafford Park industrial estate.

Privatisation of the British electricity industry saw her renamed *New Generation* in 1990, and in 2001 this was shortened to *New Gen* for her voyage to breakers at Alang. *[Paul Boot]*

Manchester's dredging fleet in colour

Top: *Donald Redford* passing Number 8 Pier, Salford on 14th May 1982.

Middle: The *MSC Irwell* of 1964 working at Eastham on 14th September 1983 with the barge *MSC No 53* alongside.

Bottom: The bucket dredger *MSC Ince*, completed in 1976, at Trafford Basin on 4th September 1984. *[All: Reg Bailey]*

DREDGING IN THE PORT OF MANCHESTER
Craig J.M. Carter

In the 113 years that have elapsed since Queen Victoria formally opened the Manchester Ship Canal dredging has been an ongoing necessity along its 39 miles and in the Mersey approach channel at Eastham. Even before the canal excavations were flooded, bucket ladder dredgers were built in the dry: Fleming and Ferguson of Port Glasgow constructing the *Bollin*, *Irk* and *Medlock* at various points along the canal bed. As the flooding progressed these vessels floated and were put to work.

Over the years much of the dredged material from the canal and the terminal docks at Salford has been pumped ashore at deposit grounds at Thelwall and Frodsham from fleets of barges towed by small tugs which attended bucket ladder dredgers. However, in 1913 the Manchester Ship Canal Company acquired a suction hopper dredger from Dutch owners. Named *Prinses Juliana*, she was built in 1910 by L. Smit en Zoon, Kinderdijk and was a steamer of 508 gross tons. She could be put to work in the Eastham approach channel or at other points in the waterway, taking her cargo of spoil out to the deposit ground in Liverpool Bay. Her hopper capacity was about 500 cubic yards and she could dredge to a depth of 45 feet. After nearly 50 years' service, during which she retained her Dutch name, she was sold in 1962 to Richard Abel and Sons Ltd., the Liverpool sand and ballast merchants,

Top to bottom: The 1893 bucket dredgers *Irk* and *Medlock* were constructed on the site of Salford Docks before water was allowed in. The *Bollin*, built by Fleming and Ferguson of Paisley, was assembled in the canal excavation between Warburton and Hollins Green and completed in 1892. The suction hopper dredger *Prinses Juliana* was photographed in the Mersey by Basil Feilden. *[Top and middle: Ted Gray collection; bottom J. and M. Clarkson]*

renamed *Peakdale* and used as a commercial sand dredger.

A plan to deepen the canal to 30 feet to allow the passage of large, deep-drafted tankers to Stanlow Oil Dock was put in hand in 1926-27 and the dredged material from this work was to be taken out to the Liverpool Bay deposit ground. For this purpose a sea-going tug and two bottom-door hopper barges were acquired. The tug *J.O. Gravel* was bought from Canadian owners in Montreal and on arrival in the Ship Canal was renamed *Clarendon*. *[See Stephen Carter's article in this issue. Ed.]* Her job was to tow the hopper barges *MSC Delta* and *MSC Gamma* to dump the spoil from the deepening work at the Liverpool Bay deposit ground. The two hopper barges, built at Renfrew in 1920, were fitted with steam steering gear and steam gear for opening and closing the bottom doors when dumping. They served the bucket ladder dredger *MSC Gowy* (442/1924) built by Fleming and Ferguson: one was moored alongside the dredger while the other was towed to sea. The tug and tow was a familiar sight in the Mersey channels for many months.

Also in 1924 the canal company took delivery of a large twin-screw grab hopper dredger named *MSC Bollin*, 1,235 gross tons, from Ferguson Bros. (Port Glasgow) Ltd. She too was employed on the deepening work as well as other jobs in the canal and daily took her dredged material out to sea. Often on a flood tide a procession of *MSC Bollin*, *Prinses*

Top: In 1962 *Prinses Juliana* was sold to Richard Abel and Sons Ltd. and renamed *Peakdale*, remaining a familiar if anachronistic sight in the Mersey until 1970 when she was sold to breakers. In August of that year she left the Mersey in tow for Faslane but put into the Menai Straits following a breakdown of her tug, *Martin Oldfield*. The tow was completed by the *Elizabeth Howard*. Demolition was completed by W.H. Arnott Young and Co. (S.B.) Ltd., Dalmuir in September.
Middle: *MSC Gowy* of 1924 at Ellesmere Port on 21st Septembe 1975.
Bottom: *MSC Bollin*, July 1951. *[Top and bottom: J. and M. Clarkson collection; middle: Ted Gray]*

Juliana and the tug *Clarendon* with a hopper barge in tow could be observed making their way downstream to the deposit ground.

With the completion of the deepening work the tug *Clarendon* and the two hopper barges were laid up in Runcorn Docks. They were reactivated from time to time when further deepening work was undertaken but in 1952 the tug was sold. The two hopper barges *MSC Delta* and *MSC Gamma* were sold in 1954 to the Westminster Dredging Co. Ltd. and each fitted with an oil engine. Renamed *WD Delta* and *WD Gamma* they served as self-propelled hoppers for that company until well into the 1960s.

One of the oldest bucket ladder dredgers working in the canal was the *Barry*, built in 1888 and still at work in the 1960s. She operated in the section between Barton and Pomona Docks with two diesel tugs of the *Daphne* class and four barges, each of 800 cubic yards capacity. This was known as *No. 3 Dredging Unit* and discharged its spoil at Thelwall Pumping Station. The bucket ladder dredger *Irk*, built in 1893, worked in the Barton to Latchford section, with one tug of the *Daphne* class and three barges, each of 500 cubic yards capacity. This was known as *No.2 Dredging Unit*, discharging at Thelwall Pumping Station. *No. 1 Dredging Unit* covered the section from Latchford to Eastham and comprised

Top: Photographed passing Birkenhead the *WD Delta* had been completed as the *MSC Delta* in 1920. Sold in 1954 to Westminster Dredging she was fitted with an engine and renamed *WD Delta*.
Middle: The tug *MSC Diana* at Eastham on 29th April 1976.
Bottom: *MSC Dawn*, a later version of the *MSC Diana*. One other dredging tug was built similar to the *Diana*, the remainder of the class like the *Dawn*. [All: J. and M. Clarkson]

35

the bucket ladder dredger *MSC Gowy*, two tugs of the *Daphne* class, two barges, each of 800 cubic yards capacity and two barges each of 500 cubic yards capacity, discharging at Frodsham Pumping Station.

The *Daphne* class diesel dredging tugs were eight in number and built between 1958 and 1960. They were named *MSC Dainty*, *MSC Daphne*, *MSC Daring*, *MSC Dart*, *MSC Dawn*, *MSC Deborah*, *MSC Diana*, and *MSC Dido*, all capable of handling the loaded dredging barges.

A new bucket ladder dredger named *MSC Irwell* was delivered in 1964, and a further similar vessel, *MSC Ince*, joined the Canal Company in 1976. By then the ancient dredgers *Barry* and *Irk* had been sold for breaking up.

Grab dredging was carried out mainly at berths. During the 1960s two grab hopper dredgers were operated by the Canal Company, *Grab Hopper No. 1* and *Grab Hopper No. 2*. They were later replaced by a single new vessel named *Donald Redford* after the Ship Canal Company Chairman from 1972 to 1985.

One of the most important aspects of dredging facing the Canal Company concerned the approach channel from Bromborough Bar to Eastham Locks. Over the years suction dredging and bucket dredging had

MSC Ince working in the Trafford Basin on 4th September 1984. *[Reg Bailey]*

Above: *MSC Grab Hopper No. 1*. *[Ships in Focus collection]*
Below: *MSC Grab Hopper No. 2* prior to her delivery by Isaac Pimblott in August 1959. *[Ships in Focus collection]*

been carried out with varying effect. For some years the introduction of a trailing suction dredger had been considered and in 1961 trials were carried out with the Westminster Dredging Company's trailer dredger *WD Seven Seas*. These trials proved that such a vessel could operate satisfactorily in the adverse conditions in this channel. A contract was signed with the Westminster company and in May 1962 their trailing suction dredger *WD Fairway* began work in the channel. She was consistently reliable and made a great improvement in the condition of the channel. In the period from 17th May 1962 to 28th February 1963 she dredged 1,230,000 cubic yards, all of which was taken out to Liverpool Bay, a distance of 22 miles away, an average return trip of 4 hours, 32 minutes.

Today the whole of the dredging operations in the Manchester Ship Canal and the approach channel have been contracted out to the Westminster Dredging Co. Ltd. using a single trailing suction dredger, the Dutch-built *WD Severn* (1,337/1974). Changed times indeed from earlier days when a fleet of different types of dredging craft were required to maintain the waterway.

Above: The grab dredger *Donald Redford* passing the pier head at Ellesmere Port in July 1981. *[Reg Bailey]*

Above: The trailing suction dredger *WD Fairway*, photographed at Eastham in 1972, revolutionised dredging in the Ship Canal approach channel when she took over from bucket dredgers in 1962. *[J. and M. Clarkson]*
Below: The trailing suction dredger *WD Severn*, seen working in the Eastham Channel on 1st May 1990, now covers all dredging requirements in the Ship Canal and its approach channel. *[J. and M. Clarkson]*

UP THE CANAL IN BLACK AND WHITE
Photographs from Nigel Farrell's collection

NICETO (above)
*William Doxford and Sons,
Sunderland, 1884; 2,811gt, 340 feet
C. 2-cyl. by William Doxford and
Sons, Sunderland*
Larrinaga's *Niceto* approaches the
entrance locks at Eastham, passing
Eastham Ferry terminal, complete
with floating pontoon and bridge.
Note also the combination of screw
and paddle tugs assisting the *Niceto*,
which was bringing a cargo of cotton
from Galveston. Larrinaga began
their service from Galveston in 1897
after considerable pressure from
Manchester interests. It was to last
until 1937.

The Spanish-flag *Niceto* had
a commendably simple career: built
for Larrinaga & Cia., Bilbao, she went
from their ownership in 1910 to
Genoese shipbreakers.

ACTON GRANGE (below)
*J.T. Eltringham and Co., South
Shields, 1907; 156gt, 100 feet
L. 2-cyl. by Hepple and Co., South
Shields*
Acton Grange and other tugs wait at
Eastham for their next tow, quite
possibly the timber-laden *Olaf* (1,890/
1897) behind them in the lock. The
tugs are moored in pairs of screw and
paddle tugs, the paddler typically

being employed as the stern tug. To
this day tugs wait at this spot,
although with declining traffic and
many ships having bow thrusters 'tug
jobs' are now infrequent. *Acton
Grange* lasted until 1951, when she
was broken up at Preston.

The late Jim Nelson
identified the other tugs in this
photograph as the screw tug *Old
Quay* (119/1907) (alongside *Acton
Grange*, with tall funnel), the screw
tug *Cadishead* (154/1917) (beyond
Acton Grange) and the paddle tug
Eccles (158/1905).

The photograph probably
dates from the 1930s: *Olaf* is in the

funnel colours of DFDS, which bought her in 1920, and used her on voyages to Manchester between 1929 and 1939. This photograph was kindly lent by Craig J.M. Carter.

FOREST HOLME (above)
J.L. Thompson and Sons, Sunderland, 1890; 2,407gt, 296 feet
T. 3-cyl. by John Dickinson, Sunderland
In April 1905 *Forest Holme* passes under Latchford Road Bridge inward bound with a cargo of wheat from the Black Sea. Her owners were Hine Brothers, unique in operating a fleet of deep-sea steamers from Maryport in Cumberland.

Forest Holme was with Hines for 22 years, but then had four owners in just five years. In 1912 she went briefly to owners in Newcastle-upon-Tyne, and a year later was put under the Greek flag as *Kardamila*. In 1916 she was sold to owners in Montevideo as *Begoña No. 4*, and somehow became the property of the Shipping Controller in 1917. It would be interesting to know under what pretext she was acquired, and whether her new name *Camphill* had any significance. However, the British government was not to have the use of her for long, as *Camphill* was torpedoed and sunk by the German submarine *U 46* on 27th July 1917 west of Ireland whilst bound from Bona to Cork with a cargo of phosphates.

TORTUGUERO (below)
Alexander Stephen and Sons Ltd., Linthouse, Glasgow, 1909; 4,161gt, 375 feet
T. 3-cyl. by Alexander Stephen and Sons Ltd., Linthouse, Glasgow
In 1902 Elders and Fyffes chose Manchester as a UK terminal for their imports, and it briefly became the major UK port for bananas. But over the years Fyffes proved fickle, and in 1911 moved their terminal to Garston, which had better rail facilities, later deserting Garston in turn for Southampton. Their *Tortuguero* approaches Irlam Locks outward bound assisted by the tug *Eastham*. On 26th June 1918 this steamer was on a voyage from the Mersey to Kingston, Jamaica when torpedoed and sunk by the German submarine *U 156*.

GERTIE (above)
Dublin Dockyard Co., Dublin, 1902, 370gt, 150 feet
C. 2-cyl. by Ross and Duncan, Govan
The Lancashire Steel Company's works at Irlam brought considerable trade to the Canal, including ore carriers. The ship visible in this photograph is more modest, the steam coaster *Gertie* of John S. Monks and Co. Ltd. Like almost all the vessels of this extensive Liverpool fleet, she was bought second hand, coming in 1911 from Alfred Rowland, who fortuitously used a similar naming scheme, so she did not need to be renamed. *Gertie* was sunk by a floating British mine off the Tuskar Rock on 8th December 1941 whilst on a voyage from Port Talbot to Waterford with a cargo of coal. Her crew was saved.

STANLEY FORCE (right)
R. Williamson and Son, Workington, 1890; 373gt, 152 feet
T. 3-cyl. by Dunsmuir and Jackson, Govan
Approaching the 45-foot-wide lock at Barton is *Stanley Force*, owned by the West Coast Shipping Co. Ltd., and managed by W.S. Kennaugh and Co. The Workington yard that constructed her from a somewhat anachronistic mixture of iron and steel had a

reputation for building to last, and *Stanley Force's* hull was good for 82 years. She was sold to London owners in 1917 and left British

registry for Italy in 1925, where she continued in service until 1972, for her final 20 years propelled by a diesel engine.

40

WHAKATANE (above)
*Hawthorn, Leslie and Co. Ltd.,
Newcastle-upon-Tyne, 1900; 5,715gt,
420 feet*
*T. 3-cyl. by Hawthorn, Leslie and Co.
Ltd., Newcastle-upon-Tyne*
In June 1904 *Whakatane* was the first
vessel loaded in Manchester for the
joint Federal-Houlder-Scottish Shire
service to Australia and New Zealand.
Ironically she belonged to none of
these companies, but to the New
Zealand Shipping Co. Ltd., which was
by then closely associated with the
Federal Steam Navigation Co. Ltd.
Note the unusually long deckhouse

built to starboard on the foredeck.
Whakatane survived the First World
War, was sold to Italian owners in
1924 to become *Moncenisio*, and was
broken up at Savona in 1929.

ESSEX (below)
*John Brown and Co. Ltd., Clydebank,
1902; 7,016gt, 460 feet*
*T. 6-cyl. by John Brown and Co. Ltd.,
Clydebank*
Seen outward bound near Barton
bridges, Federal's *Essex* may well be
on the same joint service as
Whakatane. A typical large cargo
carrier built for the Australian trade,

the twin-screw *Essex* lasted under
British ownership until 1927. She
then went under the Belgian flag, but
her ultimate owner was M.
Gumuchdjian, who may well have
been from Armenia. With
commendable brevity he renamed the
ship *Van*. She lasted until 1933 when
broken up at Bo'ness.

Use of large steamers like
Essex and *Whakatane* on Australian
services required the Manchester
Ship Canal Company to increase the
radius of the bend at Runcorn, the
tightest on the Canal, in 1909-1910.

MANCHESTER TRADER (above)
Charles J. Bigger, Londonderry, 1890;
3,318gt, 340 feet
T. 3-cyl. by McIlwaine and MacColl
Ltd., Belfast
Manchester Liner's first *Manchester Trader* clears Barton bridges inward bound. Members of the crew can be seen refixing the topmasts, despite the need to lower these again when she sails. Note also the doors in the hull, to facilitate the discharge of cattle which were an important cargo on sailings from North America.

Manchester Trader had been built for W. Johnston and Co. Ltd. as *Parkmore*, and was acquired when Manchester Liners was established in 1898. In 1912 she was sold to Norway as *Ferdinand Melsom* and after 1914 as *Kaupanger*. Despite Norway's neutrality, she was torpedoed by the German submarine *U 38* off Cartagena in December 1916 when carrying a cargo of Cardiff coal to Spezia.

STARLING (right)
Palmer's Shipbuilding and Engineering Co. Ltd., Newcastle-upon-Tyne, 1887; 804gt, 210 feet
T.3-cyl. by Palmer's Shipbuilding and Engineering Co. Ltd., Newcastle-upon-Tyne
The General Steam Navigation Company opened services from Manchester to Rotterdam and West Africa as early as 1894, but this old-established company found

competition too severe, and were forced out of the Manchester trade. Their *Starling* is pictured leaving Mode Wheel Lock on a sailing to Rotterdam. She was lost during the First World War, but not through hostile action: she collided with Wilson Line's *Tinto* (757/1911) off Treport on 7th March 1918. *Starling*

was on a voyage from London to Bordeaux with general cargo.

Palmer's shipyards are represented by two very different craft in this feature, this short-sea trader and the tanker *Ashtabula*. Was this commendable versatility, or a lack of specialisation which was to lead to this famous builder's early demise?

SAMOA (above)
William Doxford and Sons Ltd., Sunderland, 1892; 6,839gt, 445 feet T. 3-cyl. by William Doxford and Sons Ltd., Sunderland
In February 1899 Larrinaga's *Samoa* brought the largest cargo of cotton yet to Manchester, and this caused immense public interest. In this photograph of the *Samoa* entering Mode Wheel Lock assisted by the tug *Gower*, note the huge crowd on the lock wall: could anyone imagine this happening today?

Samoa was built for Crow, Rudolf and Company and passed to the Miguel de Larrinaga Steamship Co. Ltd. in 1898 without change of name. In 1901 Larrinaga took the opportunity of selling her to the United States Government as an army transport, as which she was renamed *Dix*. In 1923 she resumed commercial service as *Grace Dollar* and was broken up in Japan during 1928.

ASHTABULA (below)
Palmer's Shipbuilding and Engineering Co. Ltd., Newcastle-upon-Tyne, 1903; 7,016gt, 428 feet T. 3-cyl. Palmer's Shipbuilding and Engineering Co. Ltd., Newcastle-upon-Tyne
The tanker traffic which is now the mainstay of the Canal's activity began early, but was then concentrated on its upper reaches not, as today, on the lower. The *Ashtabula* was photographed discharging at Mode Wheel Oil Wharf during her ownership by Anglo American Oil Co. Ltd., the British subsidiary of Esso. She had been acquired in 1906 from the Northern Steamship Company of St. Petersburg for whom she had been built as the grandly-named *Graf Stroganoff*.

In 1930 *Ashtabula* found new owners as the Italian *Alabama*. Shortly after Italy entered the war she was attacked off Lake Maracaibo by the French cruiser *Jeanne D'Arc*, and run aground to avoid sinking. Such was the need for tankers that she was refloated by Venezuelan salvors, repaired and sold to the United States which had her back in service by mid-1943 as *Osmond*. She was demoted to a station tanker in March 1944 and renamed *Quiros*, but resumed the name *Osmond* when laid up after the war. She was broken up in 1947.

GENESEE (above)
Armstrong, Mitchell and Co.,
Newcastle-upon-Tyne, 1889; 2,767gt,
310 feet
T. 3-cyl. by Wallsend Slipway Co. Ltd.,
Newcastle-upon-Tyne
Another Anglo-American tanker,
Genesee was, like *Ashtabula*, a
second-hand purchase in 1899, her
original owners being pioneer tanker
operators Lane and Macandrew who
had her built as *Darial*. She later
passed to management by Galbraith,
Pembroke and Co. *Genesee* was
operated by Anglo-American until
broken up in 1924.

Genesee is being assisted
by the tug *Queen of the Mersey*. This
is the only known photo of the largest
tug owned by the Manchester Ship
Canal Company. Built in 1877 *Queen
of the Mersey* was converted from a
ferry boat, and before the Ship Canal
was opened she served the
Bridgewater Navigation Company Ltd.

CLAN LESLIE (below)
William Doxford and Sons Ltd.,
Sunderland, 1902; 3,937gt, 360 feet
T. 3-cyl. by William Doxford and Sons
Ltd., Sunderland
Clan Line was by a clear margin the
largest user of Doxford Turrets,

attracted by the considerable savings
on Suez Canal dues on sailings to
India. Judging by surviving
photographs, Clan Turrets were quite
frequent visitors to Manchester, and to
expedite their passage most had
telescopic topmasts, as seen on *Clan
Leslie* in the turning basin at
Manchester.

On 4th November 1916 *Clan
Leslie* was torpedoed and sunk by the
German submarine *UB 43* with the
loss of three of her crew. She was in
the Mediterranean on a voyage from
Bombay to London with general
cargo.

IBERIAN (above)
Sir James Laing and Son Ltd.,
Sunderland, 1900; 5,223gt, 437 feet
T. 3-cyl. by J. Dickinson and Sons
Ltd., Sunderland
Also seen in the turning basin at
Manchester, *Iberian* was a regular
visitor to the port on Frederick
Leyland's service to Boston. She was
to meet her end on such a sailing,
captured and torpedoed near Fastnet
by the German submarine *U 28* on
30th July 1915.

FLORIDA (below)
J. Cran, Leith, 1887, 28gt, 56 feet
J. Cran, Leith, 17 NHP
Florida tows a work barge near the
newly-completed Number 9 dock in
1905. She was built in 1887, but not
registered until 1891 when she was
registered in the ownership of William
Topham, one of the contractors who
constructed the Manchester Ship
Canal. The Canal company bought
her in 1894. The diminutive *Florida*
has at least two claims to fame. On
1st January 1894 she assisted the
iron barque *Grace Gibson* (542/1867),
the first deep-sea sailing ship to dock
at Manchester. On 21st May 1894
Florida also towed the royal yacht
Enchantress at the official opening of
the Canal. *Florida* was broken up in
1913.

SALLUST (above)
Sir Raylton Dixon and Company, Middlesbrough, 1898; 3,628gt, 355 feet
T. 3-cyl. by North Eastern Marine Engineering Co. Ltd., Newcastle-upon-Tyne
An early and loyal user of the Manchester Ship Canal was Lamport and Holt, with a triangular service to New York and Brazil begun in 1894. Photographed in Number 9 Dock, *Sallust* had just the one owner during her career, the Liverpool, Brazil and River Plate Steam Navigation Co. Ltd., for whom she was managed by Lamport and Holt. She was broken up at Hamburg in 1924.

SEAL (below)
A. and J. Inglis, Glasgow, 1877; 679gt, 211 feet
C. 2-cyl. by A. and J. Inglis, Glasgow
G. and J. Burns' *Seal* passes Salford Quay. *Seal* was built for the Ardrossan Shipping Company as *North Eastern*, a quirky little name which honoured a railway company. The company and its Ardrossan to Belfast sailings were taken over by G. and J. Burns in 1882, whereupon *North Eastern* was renamed *Seal*. On the opening of the Manchester Ship Canal in 1894, *Seal* and her sister *Grampus* were placed on a Glasgow to Manchester service for which their masts were cut down. Both were sold to owners in Trieste in 1907. Although she enjoyed a long career with Burns, *Seal* seems to have been

camera shy, and no other photograph of her is known despite intensive searches during the research for the Ships in Focus book 'Burns and Laird'.

MANCHESTER IMPORTER (top right)
Irvine's Shipbuilding and Dry Dock Co. Ltd., West Hartlepool, 1899; 4,028gt, 370 feet
T. 3-cyl. by W. Allan and Co. Ltd., Sunderland
In June 1904 *Manchester Importer* passes Trafford Wharf, where J.W. Carmichael's *Pontiac* (3,345/1903) is discharging timber. *Manchester Importer* remained with Manchester Liners until 1927, after which she spent six years with Greek owners as *Alexandra* before being demolished at Venice in 1933.

CIRCASSIA (right)
D. and W. Henderson and Co. Ltd., Glasgow, 1903; 7,183gt, 450 feet
T. 3-cyl. by D. and W. Henderson and Co. Ltd., Glasgow
A well-laden *Circassia* leaves Number 8 Dock on Anchor Line's service to India, a major export market for Manchester's cotton goods. Anchor's first sailing was made in January 1895. Another survivor, *Circassia* stayed with this Glasgow company until broken up at Haulbowline Dockyard, near Cork, in 1931.

FUSILIER (bottom right)
J.P. Rennoldson and Sons, South Shields, 1900; 963gt, 207 feet
T. 3-cyl. by J.P. Rennoldson and Sons, South Shields
Fisher, Renwick and Co. of Newcastle-upon-Tyne ran a successful steamer service between London and Manchester, even though the distance by sea between the two cities was perhaps three times as great as that by land. In 1902 *Fusilier* was transferred from the parent company to Fisher, Renwick and Company's Manchester - London Steamers Ltd. and re-registered in Manchester, which port of registry she retained after return to the parent company's ownership in 1912. She was almost immediately sold to Norway, where she had various owners as *Import*, *Spica II* and *Trost*, the last of which sold her to Germany in 1927. Here she was renamed *Warnow* and then *Harald Schröder* and survived the Second World War, after which she was reported as taken in reparations by the USSR, but nothing more is known of her career.

HARE (above)
Barclay, Curle and Co. Ltd., Whiteinch, Glasgow, 1886; 614gt, 216 feet
T. 3-cyl. by Barclay, Curle and Co. Ltd., Whiteinch, Glasgow
Stewart and Lowen's Dublin and Manchester Steamship Company had a regular service from the canal (where calls were made at Ellesmere Port as well as Manchester) using the former G. and J. Burns' steamer *Hare*, bought in 1899. The company promoted themselves well, and at least two different postcard views survive showing this steamer. *Hare*

served the new owners until 14th December 1917 when the German submarine *U 62* sank her in the Irish Sea whilst she was carrying general cargo between Manchester and Dublin.

HANNAH (below)
Tyne Iron Shipbuilding Co. Ltd., Newcastle-upon-Tyne, 1913; 3,697gt, 350 feet
T. 3-cyl. by Blair and Co. Ltd., Stockton-on-Tees
In May 1913 the *Hannah* is seen loading for her maiden voyage to Buenos Aires, to whose water works

is destined her cargo of pipes made by the Stanton Iron Works of Nottingham. Owned by the Rahtkens Shipping Co. Ltd. of Middlesbrough, and managed by F. Rahtkens, *Hannah* remained with this owner until 1933. She was then sold to F.W. Uittenbogaart, a Dutchman who briefly put her under the then novel Panama flag, although by 1934 she was re-registered in Rotterdam. Still named *Hannah*, she was sunk by the Spanish Nationalist submarine *General Mola* on 11th January 1938 whilst carrying grain from Antwerp to Republican Bilbao.

ARNOTT YOUNG – SHIPBREAKERS ON THE CLYDE
Part 1
Ian Buxton

Arnott, Young on the Clyde was one of the three British shipbreaking companies capable of breaking up battleships and large merchant ships, before and after the Second World War. Although only in the business for less than fifty years, they broke up some notable ships including *King George V*, *Minnekahda*, *Furious*, *Ormonde*, *Aorangi* and *Highland Monarch*.

W.H. Arnott and James Young started a coal, scrap and steel merchanting business in Glasgow's east end about 1900. Although they purchased the wreck of Admiralty tug *Ludgate* in June 1918, they did not enter the shipbreaking business until 1933, at the suggestion of W. Sloan Smith. Smith had started as an office boy before the First World War, gained experience with the Army during the war and became a partner in the 1920s. With the surplus of ships and the closure of shipyards in the early 1930s, he persuaded his partners of the good prospects of entering the ship demolition business. Initially a berth was leased at Troon harbour on the Ayrshire coast, where shipbreaking had been carried out since 1904. *Dredger No.5* was the first vessel to arrive in September 1933 at what may been part of the former J.J. King yard. Nine vessels were broken up under the Arnott, Young name.

The massive Beardmore shipyard at Dalmuir, eight miles downstream from Glasgow on the north bank of the Clyde, had closed in 1931, and its facilities were being sold off. Arnott, Young first leased part of the former East Yard, with permission from the Clyde Navigation Trust to demolish vessels of up to 400 feet on the old slipways. Ellerman's *City of Chester* (5,413/1910) was sold for £5,800, arriving at Dalmuir on 30th January 1934. She yielded 3,300 tons of steel and other materials.

W.H. Arnott, Young and Co. (Shipbreakers) Ltd. was registered on 1st February 1934 as a private limited company, with capital of only £5,000, with head office at Fullarton Iron Works, Tollcross, Glasgow. The parent company remained W.H. Arnott, Young and Co. Ltd. James Young held one-third of the shares, Smith another third, while Ronald Scott and Robert Young held a sixth each. These four plus the bookkeeper Stanley Morgan made up the Board of Directors. Arnott had dropped out much earlier. Arnott, Young also had depots at Motherwell, Manchester, Birmingham, Teesside and Bilston in Staffordshire, undertaking steel merchanting as well as dismantling work.

Seven cargo and four smaller vessels successfully demolished during 1933-4 gave Arnott, Young the confidence to bid for larger vessels. Canadian Pacific's 18,452gt liner *Empress of France* had been laid up in Fairfield's basin on the Clyde in September 1931. With little prospect of further profitable trading, she was sold to Arnott, Young on 20th October 1934 for £33,900, through brokers Turner and Hickman. She had been built in 1913 as *Alsatian* by Beardmore, and refitted by them after the First World War, so it was ironic that she returned to her birthplace to die, arriving on 24th November. Arnott, Young had now leased the east side of the fitting out basin complete with 30-ton travelling crane, with nearby workshops and offices, so could now handle ships of around 800 feet in length.

The West of Scotland Shipbreaking Co. Ltd. had operated at Troon from about 1911. Arnott, Young took them over about 1938, giving the company better access to a proper beaching ground, as the Beardmore East Yard was to be used by the Post Office as a cable ship depot. West of Scotland then operated the whole Troon facility, including Arnott, Young's former berth, as a subsidiary of Arnott, Young, although trading under their own name. After the British Shipbreakers Association was formed in 1935 to represent the industry and improve collaboration amongst British shipbreakers in the face of fierce competition from the Continent, Arnott, Young and West of Scotland constituted about 11% of an industry that scrapped each year around 120 merchant ships of some 300,000 gt, plus about 25 warships, producing around a quarter of a million tons of scrap.

The *Empress of France* was broken up where she was fitted out. *[Dr. Ian Buxton collection]*

1937 saw Arnott, Young teaming up with other British shipbreakers to bid for surplus United States Maritime Commission cargo vessels. Twenty three were purchased in the US, loaded with scrap and steamed over to the UK to feed the growing demand for steel, now that the depression had ended and re-armament started. Although Arnott, Young only broke up three (*West Hassayampa*, *City of Fort Worth* and *Arden*), they also unloaded the scrap cargoes from *Belfort* (broken up at Troon) and *West View* (Barrow) in the summer of 1938.

The BISCO years

The pre-war mix at Dalmuir consisted of good size passenger-cargo and cargo vessels, warships and local vessels like Clyde steamers, dredgers, coasters and trawlers. At the outbreak of the Second World War, virtually every ship afloat was pressed into some form of wartime service, so the supply of ships for breaking dried up. British shipbreakers turned their hand to recovering scrap from other sources such as wrecked vessels. The British Iron and Steel Corporation (usually known as BISCO) was set up to supply the British steel industry with raw materials, so they gave Arnott, Young responsibility for salvage work on the west coast of Scotland. Their most famous job was salvaging *Politician* (7,939/1921) stranded off South Uist on 5th February 1941. Some cargo was recovered before BISCO was given the job of salvaging the ship herself. They in turn subcontracted the work to Arnott, Young, so Percy Holden arrived with 16 men in BISCO's coaster *Assistance* (221/1903) on 12th May. *Politician* was lightened, patched and refloated on 20th September. But before she could be towed away for repair, the allocated tug *Marauder* was diverted, so the hull had to be beached north of Calvay Island. She was severely damaged in winter gales and her back was broken. It was decided to cut her in two, leaving the after end and number 5 hold ashore. The fore end was successfully refloated in March 1942 and towed to Port Bannatyne and then to Troon for final demolition.

The Dalmuir basin had been used for refitting warships from 1940, but in 1943 the Admiralty took over the facility to fit out escort and other naval vessels launched by Clyde shipyards which had insufficient outfitting capacity to handle relatively complex warships. New workshops were built on the east side of the basin, whose west side was already occupied by a Royal Ordnance Factory, partly using the former Beardmore engine building shops. John Brown managed the facility fitting out some twenty new hulls until the end of 1945.

In 1946 Holden joined a group of British shipbreakers surveying the shattered German shipbreaking industry. They were impressed to find more sophisticated and better equipped facilities, but most equipment was too damaged to be worth shipping back to the UK.

Arnott, Young had hoped to take over the military port at Faslane for shipbreaking, built in 1941 as an overflow for the congested port of Glasgow. But most of the deepwater facility was leased instead to their competitor Metal Industries, who had lost most of their shipbreaking facilities at Rosyth (including use of the drydocks) in 1939. Arnott, Young were pressured into taking a four-year lease on the second military port at Cairnryan in south-west Scotland, which had poor infrastructure and little skilled labour. Only seven vessels were broken up there in 1948-49, mostly under

the BISCO scheme. The hulks of the larger ships like battleship *Valiant* were towed up to Troon for final demolition.

Arnott, Young got the Dalmuir facility back in January 1946, benefiting from new cranage, shops and refurbished quays and roads. Some of the shops were used for railway wagon work, both overhaul and demolition. Furniture was made until the 1960s from good quality timber removed from the ships.

The first post-war ship to arrive for breaking on 12th January 1946 was *Empire Governor*, ex Italian *Esquilino* taken as a prize in 1940. Her hulk was towed to Troon for beaching on 18th April, by which time the uncompleted hull of the destroyer *Belleisle* had arrived from her builder's Fairfield and also gone on to Troon. Up to 1951, all the Dalmuir hulks were towed to Troon for beaching. In 1951 Arnott, Young took over the former Napier and Miller shipyard at Old Kilpatrick, one and a half miles downstream from Dalmuir. The site between the river and the railway had been used by Alex Findlay from 1941 to assemble landing craft fabricated at their Motherwell structural engineering works. The river frontage was built up with old railway sleepers and wagon frames and the slipways levelled, while deck cranes removed from cruisers were installed. Old Kilpatrick was used both for beaching and for complete demolition of smaller vessels, although larger hulks continued to be towed to Troon.

Nearly all the ships broken up between 1946 and 1963 were done under sub-contract to BISCO. BISCO would buy merchant ships on the open market and then allocate them to a suitable shipbreaker. They would take all the scrap steel, directing it to nearby works such as Colville's at Motherwell. Non-ferrous metals and re-usables like pumps and anchor cables would be sold by the breaker on behalf of BISCO on a commission basis. Admiralty vessels were not 'sold' (despite that phrase being used in many reference books) but were 'handed over' to BISCO for scrapping. After the ship had been demolished, the net proceeds (i.e. value of material recovered less breaking costs) would be returned to the relevant government department, often the Ministry of Supply rather than the Admiralty.

Notable ships broken up at Dalmuir postwar include the burned-out troopship *Empire Waveney* (ex German liner *Milwaukee*) in 1947, the battleship *Queen Elizabeth* in 1948, the bombed German liner *New York* salvaged at Kiel in 1949, and liner *Orduna* in 1951. Such was the demand for scrap that BISCO would tow ships long distances, e.g. the oil hulk *Choran Maru* from Singapore in 1949, cruiser *Shropshire* from Sydney in 1955, while *Colonial* broke her tow from Lisbon in 1950 grounding in the Firth of Clyde where she was broken up in situ by Arnott, Young. The Mulberry breakwater vessel *Bosworth* at Normandy was refloated in 1949 and towed to Dalmuir.

Most of the worn out warships had been scrapped by 1950, but from 1955 relatively young Royal Navy ships not suited to the cold war with Russia started going to the breakers, for instance the 12-year old carrier *Indefatigable* in 1956 and battleship *King George V* in 1958. Both had been laid up in the Gareloch. These two ships provided most of the workload at Dalmuir in 1957 and 1958, although both were finished off at Troon. At this time, nearly a thousand tons of scrap a week were being produced by Dalmuir and Troon combined.

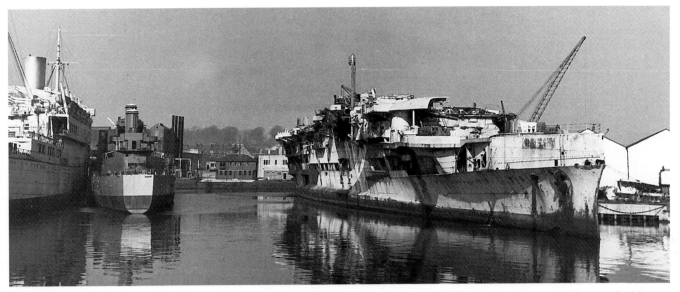

Shipbreaking resumed at Dalmuir in 1946, using the eastern side of the basin. The western side was still controlled by the Admiralty, for repairs and lay-up, including the incomplete cruiser *Tiger*. Aircraft carrier *Furious* arrived in March 1948, with island and forward part of flight deck gone by May. Her hulk was towed to Troon in June 1949 for final demolition. *[D. Macdonald]*

Battleship *Queen Elizabeth* is manouvered into the Dalmuir basin on 7th July 1948. She had been towed first to Kames Bay in the Clyde for lightening.

Five years later, *Tiger's* rebuilding has not yet started. Canadian Australasian Line's *Aorangi* arrived on 27th July 1953. The hulk of *Empire Test* is barely visible behind her. The 150-ton crane was erected by Beardmore. *[Ian Johnston]*

Passenger-cargo vessels were often allocated by BISCO to Arnott, Young. Royal Mail Lines' *Highland Monarch* is three months into demolition in this view taken on 25th July 1960. *[Brian Hargreaves]*

The scrapping of unmodernised Second World War warships continued into the early 1960s. Cruiser *Superb* has just been towed from lay-up in the Gareloch in August 1960, while demolition of *Highland Monarch* continues.

After BISCO

James Young and Sloan Smith were joint managing directors during the busy postwar period, but both died in 1954. Henry Watt, the company secretary, became chairman, an autocrat with little imagination or drive. Morgan was now the only other director, so Sloan Smith's son, Douglas Smith, joined the board. The latter was a young ambitious Cambridge engineering graduate keen to develop the company into new areas. However, Watt was the trustee for Young and Smith senior's two-thirds shareholding, and would tolerate no interference from Smith junior. He retained the position of company secretary, as well as being chairman and managing director. Watt would delay circulating important documents and then adjourn board meetings as soon as anything important arose, after having got Morgan to agree to Watt's proposals before the meeting. The company's financial position deteriorated with stocks being overvalued yet, with the winding up of the BISCO scheme after 1962, the company

An aerial view of Dalmuir taken in February 1960, with the Arnott, Young yard outlined. The vessel in the basin is aircraft carrier *Unicorn*, soon to be towed to Troon. The buildings to the west of the basin were Beardmore's engine works, later used as a Royal Ordnance Factory before being sold to Babcocks.

needed cash resources to buy ships for breaking on the open market. It was not until Watt died in 1968 (leaving the company with a large overdraft) and Douglas Smith became chairman that it was possible to find out what had really been going on, rationalise the business, close unprofitable depots like Tollcross and Motherwell, as well as Old Kilpatrick which was no longer required. A much younger board including Ian Scott, son of Ronald Scott, and Henry Brook from Sheffield, heralded a more forward-looking approach, with profits in the best years approaching a quarter of a million pounds.

The first post-BISCO ship was Ellerman's *Corinthian* (3,198/1938) purchased for £22,750 in March 1963. Her 2,674 tons of ferrous materials and 146 tons of non-ferrous metals and sundries, yielded sales income of £41,672. After breaking costs of £15,571, a profit before charging overheads was £3,351 – modest enough, even though the pound's value was some 13 times greater than today. With several of the smaller British shipbreakers closing after the wind-up of

the BISCO scheme, there was less competition for Admiralty vessels – which became the Ministry of Defence from 1964. Arnott, Young bought twelve warships at prices between £10,000 and £70,000 between 1965 and 1967, the biggest profit of £13,093 coming from their third Type 16 frigate *Termagant*, nearly one third of her purchase price. High non-ferrous metal prices helped, as they constituted around 60% of the sales income from breaking a warship.

The Scottish steelmakers still favoured ship scrap with its 5 x 2 feet sizes for their open hearth furnaces, and would pay shipbreakers an agreed premium over normal land scrap prices. Arnott, Young also broke up a dozen puffers, small steam lighters of around 80gt yielding only about 50 tons of scrap, bought for prices around £600. Two or three men could dismantle such a vessel in a couple of weeks. The oldest to go was the 64-year old *Saxon*.

The 1970s saw big changes. The shipping market collapsed in 1974, sending many ships to the breakers prematurely, especially steam tankers. Smith drew up plans for breaking up tankers too long for the 800-foot Dalmuir basin; breadth and draft when light were not a problem. He worked out that such ships could be cut in two with explosives at a Clyde anchorage, and then each half towed up to Dalmuir. But a big tanker or warship would cost around half a million pounds to buy, so finances needed to strengthened. Non-core businesses like Durham Tube and Engineering Company at Darlington were sold off. But the board was divided, some directors encouraging a reverse takeover, which would see them retained, while other directors would be sacked.

Tarmac ownership

In the event, Tarmac, strong in raw material supply, made a successful bid of £2,000,000 for the company in 1977. Brook became managing director, while a few Arnott, Young directors stayed on, including Smith. The Tarmac board agreed to invest £1,500,000 in the Dalmuir facility. Two 40-ton cranes from the recently closed Kockums shipyard in Sweden were bought, as was the 35-ton derrick crane from Charles Hill's Bristol shipyard. Two sets of hydraulic shears to reduce the chunks off the ship to furnace size were bought, although the German Henschel shears were better than the American Harris set. To

Andros Fighter, built as *Ward Hunt*, was the only Liberty ship Arnott, Young broke up, and also the last ship allocated to them by BISCO. Outboard is Ellerman's *Corinthian*, Arnott, Young's first post-BISCO ship, purchased for £22,750. *[John Hill collection]*

Arnott, Young bought several small craft from the Mersey in 1968, as resales from Northern Slipway of Dublin. Left to right on 6th September 1968 are tug *Crosby*, tank cleaning vessel *Tulipbank* (not to be demolished for another decade), tug *Alfred* behind, and tug *MSC Archer*. *[Phil Thomas]*

provide a beaching ground, the north-east corner of the basin was excavated and graded so that double bottom portions could be drawn up for final demolition in the dry.

Business boomed, with a variety of cargo vessels and tankers producing up to 1,500 tons a week. The more skilled burners could earn up to £300 a week on bonus – more than the managers! Some of the scrap was shipped in coasters to Spain's hungry electric arc steel furnaces, with the rest going to the British Steel Corporation (BSC). A bid was made for the aircraft carrier *Eagle* in 1978, but her draft of about 31 feet required the basin to be dredged at a cost of £250,000. This reduced the amount that Arnott, Young were prepared to

bid to only £300,000, so she was sold for a reputed £1 million plus to Steel Supply (Western) who broke her up at Cairnryan.

Five large and four small merchant ships were purchased in 1978 keeping the yard busy, helped by BSC's guaranteed steel scrap prices. That year saw the British shipbreaking industry producing its highest output since 1963 at 106,000 tons. But in 1980, faced with a downturn in the steel market, BSC withdrew their price support, making British yards uncompetitive with Spain and Turkey – Taiwanese prices could not be matched anyway, especially for the larger ships. Tarmac also introduced new accounting procedures for allocating overhead costs, which penalised the shipbreaking division.

Greek reefer *Mardina Importer*, built in 1958 four miles further upstream at Stephens as *Chicanoa*, arrived on 23rd June 1974. Her sister *Omoa*, ex *Changuinola*, followed the next year. Arnott, Young's 30-ton travelling crane, dating from Beardmore days, is still in use. *[Ian Johnston]*

But there were still naval vessels. Smith prepared a bid of £800,000 for *Ark Royal* in the summer of 1980. Returning from holiday, he found that not only had Tarmac refused to enter a bid to the MoD (which would have been a winning one, as she was sold for £776,000) but had decided to stop shipbreaking altogether. The Dalmuir yard closed on 4th August 1980, the last vessel to be broken up being a floating crane from Harland and Wolff at Belfast which had been lying at Cairnryan.

Final years
The year 1980 was a crunch one for British shipbreaking, with other major breakers like Shipbreaking Industries, Hughes Bolckow and Ward withdrawing from the market and selling off their sites. West of Scotland Shipbreaking had been sold in April 1980 to Ross Veitch of Girvan, who continued shipbreaking at Troon until 1986. Arnott, Young continued to process land scrap, but Tarmac sold the company to A.R. Brown, McFarlane and Co. Ltd. of Glasgow in December 1985 for £300,000. Operations moved to Rothesay Dock at Clydebank, and the Dalmuir yard was demolished by Arnott, Young itself. The basin was filled in in 1989, burying the asbestos found around most shipbreaking yards. A new private hospital was built on the site of the former Beardmore shipyard, although later converted into a hotel.

Arnott, Young was itself dissolved by Brown, McFarlane in the mid 1990s, with the latter company itself being dissolved about 2003. Thus ended a metals company whose existence had spanned about 90 years, 47 of them in shipbreaking. During this time some 220 vessels had been demolished at its Dalmuir and Old Kilpatrick yards, with a further 16 broken up at Troon and Cairnryan under the Arnott, Young name producing some 750,000 tons of recycled materials, one-third from naval vessels. Such activity will not been seen again in the UK as, in high wage countries with a limited market for re-usable materials, financial support would be needed to compete with the Indian sub-continent prices for all but small, locally-arising vessels.

To be continued.

A sad sight at Dalmuir on 29th March 1978. Former Clyde Lighthouses tender *Torch* lies half submerged after vandals got aboard. The floating sheerlegs *R.B. Telford* had to be brought in to lift her. She is alongside the hulk of *Sincerity*, while *Frankenland* is behind. *[Ian Johnston]*

SOURCES AND ACKNOWLEDGEMENTS

We thank all who gave permission for their photographs to be used, and for help in finding photographs we are particularly grateful to Tony Smith, Jim McFaul and David Whiteside of the World Ship Photo Library; to Ian Farquhar, F.W. Hawks, Peter Newall, Ivor Rooke, William Schell, George Scott; and to David Hodge and Bob Todd of the National Maritime Museum. Research sources have included the *Registers* of William Schell and Tony Starke/Rodger Howarth, The Miramar Index, *Lloyd's Register*, *Lloyd's Confidential Index*, *Lloyd's War Losses*, *Mercantile Navy Lists*, *Marine News* and *Shipbuilding and Shipping Record*. Use of the facilities of the World Ship Society's Central Record, the Guildhall Library, the Public Record Office and Lloyd's Register of Shipping are gratefully acknowledged. Dr Malcolm Cooper is thanked for checking Second World War losses, and David Asprey, John Bartlett, Louis Loughran, Bill Schell and John D. Stevenson for additional research. Particular thanks also to Heather Fenton for editorial and indexing work, and to Marion Clarkson for accountancy services.

British and Continental
Colin Turner wrote a history of the company which appeared in 'Sea Breezes' along with a fleet list in that journal's style. By coincidence, another 'Record' contributor, Geoff Holmes, wrote about his service with the company in 'Ships Monthly' for July 1990, and some of his memories are also incorporated.

The tale of an MSC tug
In researching this article much help was given by Paul Andow, David Asprey, Tom Carreyette, Gabriel Drew of the Manchester Record Office, Ted Gray, Alan Hughes, Mac Mackay and Piet van Damme.

Up the Canal in black and white
As well as sources listed above for details of ships' careers, Farnie DA 'The Manchester Ship Canal and the Rise of Manchester' (Manchester University Press, 1980) was consulted as probably the only book dealing with the trade of the Ship Canal, rather than its promotion and construction.

Up the Canal in colour
Thanks to Reg Bailey, Paul Boot, Nigel Bowker and Eddie Jackson for providing slides, and an additional thank you to Paul Boot for digitalisation and image optimisation.

PALM LINE FOLLOW-UP

Deckhouses and delays

My time as an apprentice ship draughtsman with Short Brothers, Pallion Shipyard, Sunderland, ended in 1951 on completion of a three-year naval architecture sandwich course at the local technical college, and I returned to the drawing office from this to await call up for National Service. Not knowing how long this waiting time might be, the Chief Draughtsman was reluctant to entrust me with a task of any magnitude, consequently I 'filled-in' with a range of odd jobs, and references to *Africa Palm* and *Burutu Palm* in 'Record 35' reminded me that these included preparing drawings for the small deckhouses built on the poop of these vessels. National Service did, in fact, claim me shortly afterwards, long before construction of the pair commenced, and it is only by reference to photographs that I could subsequently admire the results of my design skills.

Whether Palm Line accepted Short's explanation for the delays in completion of the vessels or not, there is no doubt that shortage of materials was a real problem for all the British shipyards at this time. In his book, 'The History of North East Shipbuilding', author David Dougan highlights this, and quotes Cyril Thompson, Managing Director of J.L. Thompson, who pointed out that with steel supplies limited to 60% of requirements, 'wholesale unemployment would soon be inevitable'. Owners were cancelling orders because no fixed delivery date could be promised and, although there was an abundance of work available, new contracts were not being booked because of this uncertainty concerning completion dates, and also final cost, because in those days most contracts were not being placed on a 'fixed price' basis. It was not just shortage of steel which was causing problems: another Sunderland shipbuilder, Bartram and Sons, was late delivering an Argentinian cargo liner because of a lack of cabin door knobs!

JOHN LINGWOOD, 52 Nursery Road, Sunderland SR3 1NT

Masts and other matters

'Record' 35 not only carried two references which are worth a response but both concerned companies in which I served during my years at sea. The subject is the choice of masts by those two lines.

The adoption of the bipod mast by Palm Line was a more practical measure. It not only dispensed with the mast shrouds but also the need for separate ventilator housings. When you are loading long, heavy logs, especially in a sea anchorage, you want the main deck to be well free of any targets for careless winch drivers. Elder Dempster introduced the bipod to the West African trade in 1957 so that may well have influenced Palm but then Elders returned to conventional masts for their buildings contemporaneous with Palm's 'I' class and only returned to bipods with their last conventional ships. Incidentally, one advantage of the bipod mast was that, with the right gang of Krooboys, you could rig derricks so as to pass cargo that needed shifting straight out of number 2 'tween deck, through the legs and down into number1 'tween deck. Mind you, I nearly had a fit when I saw what they were up to at first!

Strange how satisfying it can be to look more closely even at ships that one knew intimately. I'd almost forgotten our habit of hanging off the pilot ladder from the samson posts immediately next to the bridge front. This allowed the ladder to be rigged and unrigged by just one watch keeper but you had to make sure that, after use, it was well lashed in, otherwise there were complaints from those with bridge front cabins if the ladder was able to flap freely against any adjacent steelwork.

Also note the two photographs on page 139. They are probably separated by about a decade or so. The *Ibadan Palm* shows two-fold purchases hoisted on the six fifteen-ton derricks, the black paint used makes them especially clear. This rig is absent on the *Ilorin Palm* even though the earlier use of champagne colour on the derrick blocks makes it more difficult to interpret. The reason for the difference is obsolescence of the cargo gear (I mentioned this briefly in my account) which meant that you had to be ready to change to a swinging derrick arrangement quickly as unit loads increasingly exceeded the 2.5 ton capacity of union-purchase rig. Small but telling details!

Of course we 'Record' customers are never completely satisfied so I'll just regret that the full glory of Palm would have benefited from your colour treatment!

JOHN GOBLE, 55 Shanklin Road, Southampton SO15 7RG

Lagosian

Predecessor to Palm Line, the United Africa fleet included an interesting miscellany of second-hand tonnage. One ship which drew my attention was the *Lagosian*, ex *Melmay*, which was built at Greenock in 1930. The ship looked like an enlarged timber carrier and was built for T.L. Duff of Glasgow, who parted with the ship within two years. I

The *Lagosian* off Greenwich on 17th September 1933: note the sailing barge passing astern of her. *Lagosian* was torpedoed by the German submarine *U 159* in position 25.35 north by 15.43 west during a ballast voyage from Algiers and Gibraltar to Takoradi in convoy RS 3. [R. Snook/F.W. Hawks]

wonder if United Africa employed the ship as a log carrier, because they had no other ships of that type and used conventional cargo ships in the log trade.

The *Lagosian* had a short career, being torpedoed off the Canary Islands in March 1943, but prior to that she was set on fire and severely damaged by German aircraft off Peterhead in September 1940. My first encounter with the *Lagosian* was later in 1940, when the ship was dry docked at North Shields in a deplorable state, which took many months to repair. It was one of those cases where a wreck was rebuilt solely because of the demand for anything that would float.

JOHN B. HILL, The Hollies, Wall, Hexham, Northumberland NE46 4EQ

PUTTING THE RECORD STRAIGHT

Letters, additions, amendments and photographs relating to features in *any* issues of 'Record' are welcomed. Communications by e-mail are acceptable, but senders are asked to include their postal address. Letters may be lightly edited.

British yard, Greek corrections

May I comment on Ships in Focus 'Record' 36, and in particular on the article and photographs pursuant to George Foustanos' monumental work 'Kings of the Oceans'? I refer to the captions for photographs of the *Aghios Nicolaos* (page 233), *Yannis* (page 234), as well as of *Dona Margarita* on the same page.

Firstly, *Aghios Nicolaos*. According to the caption, the design of the forerunner of this vessel, our *Kassos* was 'credited to Captain Nicholas Rethymnis'. This suggestion was indeed made in the 'Motor Ship' in 1939 and as far as I know was never commented upon; may I, however, put your long-distant source and indeed your own columns right. *Kassos'* design - at least as regards the owners' contribution to it - was a collegiate affair and rested between the Kassos Steam Navigation Co. Ltd. partners, my grandfather Captain Michael Pnevmaticos, and my great uncles Captains Stathes Yannaghas, Nicholas Rethymnis and Minas Rethymnis. In fact reference to previous new buildings of the same partnership (*Hadiotis* of 1929, *Themoni* of 1929 and *Themoni* of 1938) clearly show the hull design lineage leading to *Kassos* herself.

Secondly, according to the caption, the *Aghios Nicolaos* entered service under the Panamanian flag. This is not correct; she was registered in Syra, Greece upon delivery and hoisted the Greek flag from the start. Thirdly, to write that it was Minas Rethymnis who returned to Doxfords, as you do in this caption, is to wrongly attribute decision-making of the partnership to one of its members, and more about this below. Now to *Yannis*. Again you attribute to Minas Rethymnis 'and his associates' in your caption to the above vessel, decisions in which he was hardly involved; more about this ship below. It is perhaps appropriate for me to give your readers the procedure which was followed when my grandfather Captain Michael Pnevmaticos (for it was chiefly he, as the senior partner, rather than Captain Nicholas Rethymnis) ordered a ship. Common to all dry cargo new buildings of the partnership from 1929 up to and including *Aghios Spyridon* in 1957, there was one thread, and this was the chemistry between Dr. J. Ramsay Geddie and my grandfather. Geddie as a young man had been at Northumberland Shipbuilding Ltd. when the first R&K new ship was built (the aforesaid *Hadiotis* of 1929), and thereafter oversaw the first and second *Themoni* of 1929 and 1938 and Dr. Geddie was at Doxfords for the *Kassos* in 1939. After the war, the procedure was a gentlemanly one. Every winter Dr. Geddie and his wife Edie would spend some weeks with my grandfather in Monte Carlo and, more often than not, a ship would result. If technical details needed to be clarified, then Dr. Geddie's number 2, Mr. Clem Stephenson, would come down with his wife Babs, and the issues would be thrashed out. The resultant contract would not be more than a few pages and both my grandfather and my father always praised Doxfords for being fair and sensible in the resultant product. *Yannis*, for instance, turned out to be exceptionally fast - 21 knots or so on trials, more economical at service speed than contracted, with 500 tons more deadweight, all without a penny extra charged as a result; contemporary shipyards, please take note of how to handle a long-term relationship!

To turn now to the Chandris new buildings, and to the caption for the photograph of *Dona Margarita*, also on page 234. My grandfather's first daughter, Myrto, married Dimitri J. Chandris and both he (affectionately known as Mimis) as well as his brother, Anthony Chandris, were regularly in Monte Carlo over the winter. Inevitably they together with Dr. Geddie were all under my grandfather's mantle every day and, lo and behold, as you rightly state, five Chandris ships resulted for Doxfords between 1956 and 1959 from that source as well. Dr. Geddie's task became more difficult when Basil Mavroleon acquired Austin and Pickersgill, because as a cousin and R&K partner together with the Kulukundis, Pnevmaticos and Rethymnis families, relationships were in place for Austins to perhaps hi-jack prospective orders. Mr. Mavroleon spent the winters in Monte Carlo as well, where his yacht *Radiant* was based, and was also in my grandfather's company every day. In the event, though, Doxfords never lost out to Austin and Pickersgill, but Mr. Mavroleon did wrest, at a desperate time for his British yard, the contract to build the *Vasilios R* from the Japanese. At the very last minute, thanks to Basil Mavroleon's frantic intervention, this time largely with Captain Nicholas Rethymnis on a very shaky transAtlantic telephone line, Austins agreed to build this ship to the Japanese designs and at the Japanese price; the resultant quality of the British-built ship, at least initially, was not a particularly happy one and she was in fact rejected on trials pending modifications and strengthening. This extreme cost-paring approach during construction, however justified in theory, was to lead to a return to Doxfords for *Yannis* and *Marigo R*.

May I now clarify the *Yannis*? She was a joint venture between Pnevmaticos and Chandris interests and as you rightly state was managed by the Chandris organisation and not by Rethymnis and Kulukundis as part of this one-off enterprise. She carried Kassos colours to reflect the equity in the ship, but just to restate what I say above, Minas Rethymnis had nothing whatsoever to do with her, other than to be a most welcome guest at the ship's launching by my grandmother - at which he was, as always, the life and soul of the party. Lastly, as to the ship name and details tabulation on page 232, sorry to be pedantic, but the *Aghios Spyridon* had a 6- and not a 4-cylinder Doxford main engine. I hope the background to these ships has been of interest.

MICHAEL MATANTOS, Kanari 1, GR-18537, Piraeus

Springwell Shipping

In 'Record' 36 a question is raised about Springwell Shipping Co. Ltd., previous owner of the steamer *Springfjord*. According to my sources, the original company, Springfjord Shipping Co. Ltd., was bought by the famous Norwegian shipowner Hilmar Reksten who was during 1942 working for Norwegian authorities in Nortraship, based in London. One vessel that belonged to the company had the Norwegian-like name *Springbjørn* – the suffix 'bjørn' meaning bear.

TORE NILSEN, Sandbakkveien 67, N-7072 Heimdal, Norway.

Plassy, the wreck on the telly

Wrecked on Innisheer, one of the Aran Islands, *Plassy* ex-*Peterjohn* (Page 203, 'Record' 36) attained some fame (or should it be notoriety?) as the 'Father Ted' ship. This TV series, about three dysfunctional Irish priests on the fictional Craggy Island, begins with a helicopter coming in from the sea and approaching the island. As it sweeps over the coast, a derelict wreck is a prominent feature. The ship is the *Plassy*, now driven by gales well above high-water mark subsequent from her original grounding site. She is in deplorable condition, with her back broken just behind the bridge, and covered with rust. Colour photographs of the wreck appeared in 'Sea Breezes' for November 2002 and November 2003. As she is not subject to any wave action, the hulk may well remain for many years to come, until it succumbs to rust.

TONY SMYTHE, 35 Avondale Road, Rayleigh, Essex SS6 8NJ
Thanks also to regular correspondent A.D. Frost of Sunderland for writing to us about Plassy's *television appearances.*

Putting 'Record' 13 straight

I feel that some amplification of a letter from Colin J. Francis on page 39 of 'Record' 13 may be of interest.

I was an apprentice on *Rakaia* at the time and remember the incident very clearly. The engine breakdown occurred in mid-October 1957 and the vessel was drifting for about three days whilst the engineers cleared up the damage and isolated the damaged cylinder.

Colin Francis makes mention of repelling boarders from a Watts, Watts vessel. The vessel in question was the *Woolwich* which had altered course to see if we required assistance, no doubt hoping for a nice little salvage job, and arrived on the scene flying the appropriate signal. Our master, Captain H.N. Lawson RNR, wishing to be polite, ordered the reply 'no thank you', consisting of two hoists, N and OVF. Unfortunately, when the second hoist went up, it read FVO meaning 'expedite' and this caused a flurry of activity around the *Woolwich*'s lifeboat until the error was discovered.

I can assure Colin that, as one of 36 hungry apprentices, I have no recollection of going without a shower or my eggs and bacon for breakfast.

Rumour had it that the master received a bonus of £350 with others on a sliding scale; but I do know that apprentices under 18 received £8 10s and those over, £10.

Anyone wishing to read a report on the breakdown and subsequent sail-assisted voyage can find Chief Officer J.T. Varney's report at www.rakaia.co.uk under the heading 'Jury sails in the North Atlantic'.

JOHN R. WOODLEY, 18 Brown Street, Geelong East, Victoria 3219, Australia

Department of Correction

On page 185 of 'Record' 31, does not the author mean *Sociality*? She was fitted with a special onboard pump to discharge bulk cement which was loaded at West Thurrock for Leith. I know, I was on this vessel as an E.D.H. in the summer of 1963.

RICK COX, 113 Heol Carnau, Ely, Cardiff CF5 5NG

Minor details on page 242 of 'Record' 36: the *Caslon* is inbound in 1962 to Dalhousie New Brunswick not Pugwash, Nova Scotia; and *Baskerville* was outward bound from Dalhousie.

JOHN LOW, 1500 du Bocage, St. Bruno, Quebec, J3V 4M6

Bartrams-built

I was delighted to see again the two pictures of the Bartram-built *Pussur* and *Ocean Endurance* in 'Record' 36, for as a young man in the early 1960s I was Fitting Out Manager on both of them. I remember particularly the *Ocean Endurance*, as with provision for 20 first class passengers and 150 pilgrims, she had substantially more in terms of accommodation than the usual dry cargo vessels and reefers for Blue Star Line and New Zealand Shipping Company we were accustomed to build at that time.

Shortly after that in 1967 I was appointed Yard Manager of the Bartram yard at the very start of the SD14 programme. We set ourselves a target of six launches and

completions each year for the first few years; the very first one being *Mimis N. Papalios* which, due to a misunderstanding on the launch platform, was very nearly launched without the bottle of champagne being smashed on her bows, the lady concerned swinging and hitting a moving target, the launch button having been inadvertently pressed prematurely by someone who shall remain nameless.

I was therefore very interested also to see the piece by John Lingwood in 'Record' 32 and the series of photographs which have come to light which must have been taken by the yard photographer Denis Gillan or his assistant Wally. From examination in detail, they were taken some years into the Bartram SD14 programme shortly after I had left the company in 1972.

Looking at these photographs taken in the mid 1970s of construction of what were then called Liberty ship replacements, I am struck by the similarity with pictures I have illustrating construction techniques in the California Shipbuilding Corporation yard in 1942 at the height of the original Liberty ship building programme. The scale is different of course, for they were building at least a ship a week whereas Bartrams launched one SD14 every eight weeks. The Americans wore aluminium safety hats and used umbrellas to shade the welders from the sun, whereas at Bartrams the struggle was to shelter from the driving North Sea rain nine months of the year.

ROBERT S. HUNTER, 2 Westoe Hall, South Shields NE33 3EG

British-built Pakistani tankers

Apropos the interesting article and photographs in recent 'Records' concerning UK-built Pakistani-flag vessels, I noticed that there was no reference to tankers. Back fifty years or more when I joined Shell's chartering department I can recollect at least two UK-built tankers under the Pakistani flag. I believe the reasons for Shell employing these vessels was as a quid pro quo for their involvement in a new refinery in Karachi to be built for the Pakistan National Oil Company.

The first vessel, *Mushtari*, was a veteran of about 8,000 tons deadweight. Not really suitable even then for Shell's trade, my recollection is that, fortunately for Shell, she spent most of her time repairing and hence off hire. She was replaced by a second *Mushtari* which was a 16,000-ton tanker built as *Empire Collins* and later owned by Salvesen as *Southern Collins* for their whaling expeditions.

Shell and other oil majors were often obliged to take national flag tonnage for oil production, refining, marketing, cabotage or other political reasons.

JIM SWAN, Flat 8, 39 Courtfield Gardens, London SW5 0PJ
The first Mushtari *was built in 1917 as* British Light. *She became the Royal Navy's* Olwen *in 1937, moving to Pakistan in 1949. She was broken up at Karachi in 1959. Her successor was built in 1942 by Sir J. Laing and Sons Ltd., Sunderland. After carrying the names* Empire Collins *and* Southern Collins, *in 1956 she became* Cassian Sailor, *and ran as* Mushtari *for Gulf Steamships Ltd., Karachi from 1960 until broken up locally in 1964. Ed.*

It's not farewell to *Berga*

Although it was generally believed that the *Berga* ('Record' 33) was to be scrapped (even 'Lloyd's Shipping Index' listed her contact as 'Pakistan Breakers' and sailing from Falmouth for Gadani Beach) it is pleasing to report that she has escaped that fate, for the time being at least, following a sale for further trading. It was noted that she made a southbound transit of the Suez Canal on 8th April 2006 renamed *Novanoor* (Sierra Leone flag), but the exact date of her sale to new owners, United Arab Emirates-based Hussain Hindas Khalifa and Salam J.A. Ali, has not been established. She was later reported at Aqaba and subsequently loaded a cargo of bagged cement in India. On 27th November 2006 she arrived at Umm Qasr, Iraq and more recently at Kandla on 11th April 2007, sailing three days later.

NIGEL JONES , 12 Powys Drive, Dinas Powys, CF64 4LN

The *Mushtari* of 1917 (above), originally the *British Light*, seen at Mombasa in 1957. *[Ships in Focus]*

Mike West of Newton Abbot has kindly pointed out that the feature on British-built ships owned in Pakistan omitted the *Ocean Ensign* (below) of the Transoceanic Steamship Co. Ltd. She was completed by William Hamilton and Co. Ltd. at Port Glasgow in December 1945 as the Y-type steamer *Empire Goodwin* and in 1947 was sold to Denholms as *Garvelpark*. Pakistani ownership came in 1958 and lasted until early 1971 when she was demolished at Gadani *[Ships in Focus]*

USS *St. Tudno?*

Following the publication of 'The Liverpool and North Wales Steamship Company' by Ships in Focus, Bill Schell kindly sent an entry from an encyclopedia of US Navy craft which documents a little-known aspect of the career of St. Tudno of 1891.

She was requisitioned by the Admiralty in 1914 as a troop transport, and was loaned to the United States Navy from about the time of the Armistice until 21st August 1919. Apparently known simply as Tudno, there is no record of her being commissioned and she does not appear in contemporary lists, although her commanding officer was Lieutenant William J. Brown of the United States Naval Reserve. She performed valuable service at Brest in the effort to bring US troops to the UK for repatriation to the US, ferrying troops from the docks to waiting ships which included the Leviathan and battleship USS New Jersey, and Cunard's Aquitania to the armoured cruisers USS Frederick and Huntington. During the course of this service some important persons trod her decks, albeit only briefly. President Woodrow Wilson and his party came ashore on her from the George Washington on 13th December 1918 as the President prepared to take part in the Paris Peace Conference. The Tudno took Wilson and his party back to the George Washington on 15th February 1919.

The Tudno's last troop-ferrying duty came on 12th August 1919 when she took 1,400 men out to the transport

Powhatan. On 16th August she left Brest for Southampton and there, on the morning of 21st August, she was handed back to the British Admiralty.

More on *Loch Etive*

Reference to *Loch Etive* in 'Record' 36 reminds me of some arrangements used to serve the British Aluminium Company whose plants at Kinlochleven opened in 1908 and at Fort William in 1929. They were remote from the company's markets, the criterion being the plentiful power supply to produce aluminium.

J. and A. Gardner and Co., Glasgow owned quarries at Bonawe on Loch Etive, and used their own coasters to ship stone to Glasgow. They had few cargoes when sailing north until British Aluminium came into the picture. Gardners then obtained open annual charters which allowed them to load any of their ships which would otherwise have sailed north in ballast, although British Aluminium were free to use their own vessels or charter elsewhere.

Cargoes to Kinlochleven or Fort William included coke, coal, pitch and fireclay from Glasgow; coal from Ayrshire or the Bristol Channel; and alumina from Larne. The aluminium was shipped to Glasgow and Liverpool.

DAVID BURRELL, 6 Glaisnock View, Cumnock, Ayrshire KA18 3GA

RECORD REVIEWS

GREEK PASSENGER LINERS by William H. Miller
96-page landscape-format softback published by Tempus
Publishing Limited at £19.99

The forward to this book describes it as a tribute to many Greek passenger ships of the past half century, and there are photographic representations of some 140 vessels, including 36 in colour, fronted by an atmospheric, but unattributed, painting of the *Queen Frederica*. Most have reproduced well on good quality art paper, but a few are fuzzy and some have been reduced so drastically that the bows and/or sterns have been cropped out of the picture. They have come from a relatively limited group of admittedly well-known cameramen, and several vessels are shown only in their non-Greek form, even though it should not have been a problem to trace more relevant material. Bill Miller has previously co-operated with Carmania Press to produce titles (for instance, 'Passenger Liners - Italian Style') for specific countries, but anyone expecting a comparable product will be disappointed. The coverage of companies is far more uneven with a concentration on better-known vessels which have already been featured exhaustively in the hobby press. It is difficult to escape the feeling that the author is out of his comfort zone, relying on a view from across the Atlantic, augmented with interesting snippets provided by retired Lloyd's Register ship surveyor Arthur Crook and a few memories from Greek cruise ship officers. Whilst accepting that ownership in the complex world of Greek shipping is often somewhat mysterious, this book does little to unravel how companies are formed and associated. There do seem some strange selections; thus, Gerry Herrod would be surprised to find Orient Lines included, presumably on the strength of *Marco Polo* being transformed at the Neorion yard (although this detail is not mentioned); Home Lines were treated as an Italian company in Bill's earlier book, even though the principal owner was Greek, so becomes a significant entry here as well; on this basis, you could expect more than just one passing reference to the Portuguese Arcalia Shipping with George Potamianos at the helm. On the other hand, the flagship Greek company of the late 1990s, Royal Olympic Cruises (ROC), surely warrants more attention than a few lines at the end of the Epirotiki and Sun Lines histories, and the Louis Cruises' section is silent concerning the period of majority shareholding in ROC. Smaller companies get sketchy treatment, mostly by captions within a photo feature; with several ships mentioned in each caption, it is sometimes difficult to tell which vessel is depicted. Without an index making connections is a problem. For example, one caption describes *Constellation* of Kavounides having a later life as *Salamis Glory* but she is illustrated as *Regent Spirit*; go to the history of Regency Cruises, and there is a mention of *Regent Spirit*, but not *Salamis Glory*. The short passage on Ambassador Cruises omits any reference to *Romantica,* although ownership is so identified within the Chandris pages. Proof reading has failed to spot other discrepancies, for example Efthymiades' *Minos* is incorrectly described as sailing later for the Lesvos company; the accompanying photo clearly shows the markings of Minoan Lines for whom she did operate for ten years. The author seems to have gone along with the inclusion of a handful of passenger-carrying vehicle ferries on domestic service, mainly those equipped with side doors such as the converted tankers and the ex-Bibby liners, possibly because the losses of the *Heleanna* and the *Heraklion* led directly to the demise of their owners. But it is again an oddity that the stern-loading ferry *Castalia* is chosen for Hellenic Med Lines in preference to the ground-breaking *Egnatia*, perhaps because the former eventually became a casino boat in US waters. Overall, this volume is frustrating because it could have been so much better with a bit more research and care, and the decent bibliography at the back of the book suggests that a more definitive study of Greek passenger shipping is still awaited.

Roland Whaite

JOHN HOLMAN & SONS LTD: A FAMILY BUSINESS OF
SHIPBUILDERS, SHIPOWNERS AND INSURERS FROM
1832 by David B. Clement
200-page A5 softback published by the Topsham Museum
Society at £12.00

The Holman family were one of a considerable number of west country shipowners who made the successful transition from sail to steam, moving their operations from Topsham in Devon to London in order to manage a fleet of tramps. They also embraced shipbuilding and insurance, the latter ensuring their survival in business to the present day. This book attempts to cover all three aspects of the Holman business with varying degrees of success. It is probably best viewed as a work of local and family history, which also aims to chronicle the ships which the Holmans built and either owned outright or in which they had shares. It is very much local in the sense that the compilers appear not to have strayed far beyond local sources, both of documentary and of illustrative material, and therein lie its weaknesses. For instance, details of the tramp steamers include such information as the size of the ballast tanks (available from registration certificates), but rarely given are details of the ships' subsequent careers, and often even their fate whilst in Holman ownership is vague. This may be excused for the early sailing ships, but for the steamers the additional information is readily available, not just in reference books like 'Lloyd's Register' but also in publications such as the Starke/Schell Registers. Illustrations also seem solely from local sources: for instance, they include the brass plate from a builder's model in Topsham Museum (but strangely not the model herself). However, there are no photographs of any of the steamers in Holman ownership, yet at least the *Gertor* of 1892 and the *Armstor* of 1909 were photographed, as were the ships of the Dene Shipping Co. Ltd. in which the Holmans had shares. The reviewer also questions the wisdom of reproducing barely-legible pages from ledgers and other contemporary documents.

There is much information here, but it is often served up unprocessed. For instance, a letter from the master of the steamer *Enmore* describes how he successfully filled his steamer with cotton bales in New Orleans, but there is no indication of the overall trading pattern of the steamers other than a note that some carried indentured labourers to the West Indies. Again, available records would have supplied this data. The latter chapters on the current and indeed (surely unique for a history book) future activities of the company in insurance read like press releases: everything is wonderfully successful. Proof reading and fact checking could have been better: we read of an owner from 'Ulveston Port, Cheshire'. If this was indeed Ulverstone, it was certainly not in Cheshire, but in north Lancashire. At least one imaginary steamer appears: there never was an *Ocean Pilgrim* of 1936. There was an *Ocean Pilgrim* of 1942 which is listed.

The reviewer could well be judged harsh in his criticisms, as histories of modest companies like this are rare enough to deserve to be treated like delicate flowers. The author and the museum publishers are indeed to be praised for undertaking the work (which is well printed and very attractively priced), but surely a job like this, if worth doing, is worth doing well. As organisations like the World Ship Society have shown in the past, an amateur publication does not have to be amateurish.

Roy Fenton

ATMOPLÍA TON OINOUSSÍON (OINOUSSIAN
STEAMSHIPS) 1905-1940 by George M. Foustanos
256-page A4 hardback published by the Oinoussian Maritime
Museum at £69.50

The tiny island of Oinoussai, lying off the coast of Chios and scant miles from the mainland of Asia Minor, has – as author George Foustanos tells us – a centuries-old tradition of seamanship. Despite there being no Oinoussian registry (a fact seemingly belied by the cover photo of the 1911-built *Antonis G. Lemos* proudly but quite unofficially displaying the name of her home island on her counter!), Oinoussai had a disproportionately important effect on Greek, and world, shipping throughout the twentieth century. It was home to the Lemos, Pateras and Hadjipateras families, some of whose members banded together in 1905 to purchase the *Marietta Ralli* of 1891, which was to become the first steamer owned in the island. Joined a little later by the Lyras family, they went on to constitute one of the most eminent shipping dynasties of recent times. Kinship and intermarriage between the families was rife, and the legal ownership of many of the ships was consequently often complex; Foustanos details the precise shares held in each individual vessel, and presents us with a fine array of family portraits of the shareholders (who in many cases were also masters and officers of the ships), their spouses, children and relatives, as well as landscapes and harbourscapes of Oinoussai itself. There is also a fair amount of realia – newspaper cuttings, telegrams, insurance correspondence, share certificates; a bilingual text gives potted biographies of the ships, and there is an appendix detailing those ships lost in both world wars, along with the circumstances of their loss and the names of the personnel who perished with them. This is all fascinating stuff; but for me, as ever, it is the quality of the pictures which makes or breaks a book of this kind, and it has to be said that in this regard it is consistently excellent. Each ship has a double-page spread devoted to her, an average of slightly over half of each spread being pictorial matter. Some of this is the peripheral material already alluded to, but nearly every ship is represented by at least one photograph (or painting, in those cases where no photo could be found), and many by two or more. Somewhat over 100 ships are accorded this treatment, the vessels being arranged chronologically in the order of their acquisition by Oinoussian owners. However esoteric this may all sound at first hearing, there is a wealth of interest here for the lover of twentieth-century British merchant shipping, as the overwhelming majority of the vessels in these pages are British-built: built, in a few cases, for their Greek owners (Hellenic owners, I should perhaps say, as Foustanos invariably uses this adjective for preference), but in most cases bought second-hand. Several originated in the fleets of major British liner companies – Booth, Pacific Steam, Prince, Furness, Elder Dempster, Houlder, Bank Line – but more commonly they were purchased from tramping companies, and admirers of that most unjustly disregarded vessel, the British tramp, will have a field-day here. Hain; Hogarth; Common; Dalgliesh; Reardon Smith; J. and C. Harrison; MacLay, McIntyre; Burrell; Dunlop; Radcliffe; Farrar Groves; Seager – ships from these and many other more obscure tramping fleets are represented here, in quite a few cases being shown in the livery of their British owners when no photo of them in their Hellenic incarnation was to be found. The same is even true of a couple of the ex-liner-company vessels, there being (for example) excellent likenesses of Booth's *Dominic* and *Dunstan* of 1895/1896. I need hardly say that when the ships are portrayed in the service of their Oinoussian owners, they are, as usual, a joy to behold, the pride in maintenance and appearance manifested by these family concerns being justifiably renowned.

We in this rather bigger island have a great deal to learn from the Oinoussians. *Oinoussian Steamships*, a most impressive and authoritative volume, was commissioned from George Foustanos by the Oinoussian Maritime Museum; a visit to the National Maritime Museum at Greenwich recently revealed scarcely a passing mention of the tramps to which London, perhaps more than any other port, was once home. The picture of the maritime past portrayed by the NMM is not the reality that I remember, in which tramps provided a livelihood to hundreds of thousands of people and indirectly affected the lives of millions: where is one now to find a likeness of a British tramp, outside, that is, of that honourable exception – the pages of 'Ships In Focus Record'? A great disservice is being done to future generations in this country by the purveyance of a revisionist version of maritime history, in which there is only sail, navy, passenger traffic and slavery, and the mainstay of this island's existence, the cargo vessel (colliers and coasters are also pretty well invisible in the NMM) is airbrushed out of the picture. It is good to observe that the Oinoussians, at least, accord to the trade of their recent forebears the acknowledgement and respect that it undoubtedly deserves.

Christy MacHale

CARGO SHIPS: A COLOUR PORTFOLIO by David L. Williams and Richard de Kerbrech
PASSENGER LINERS IN COLOUR by David L. Williams and Richard de Kerbrech
Both 80-page hardbacks published by Ian Allan at £14.99

These are landscape picture books aimed squarely at the market for nostalgia. Both follow similar formats concentrating on 1950s to mid-1970s with photographs of British-owned vessels, organised alphabetically by shipping company, complemented with standard data about each ship and a short narrative, mostly about her history.

The photographs are mostly by Kenneth Wightman or from the collection of Mick Lindsey. Some are fine images with fair to good reproduction. Others such as *Southern Cross* ('Passenger Liners in Colour', page 68) and *Reina del Mar* (ibid, page 76) disappoint; apart from unfortunate cropping it is difficult to tell whether image or reproduction is at fault. Reproducing atmospheric dock scenes, with tugs and lighters, rather than solely ships underway is to be applauded. But why include so many small images, about a sixth of the total, where the text space can be larger than the photo? These are too small to enjoy and make the presentation very messy.

Some captions are quite lengthy and the balance between text and photo might sometimes be questionable. Some narratives are taut and factual; but *City of Birmingham* ('Cargo Ships', inside front cover) is not 'pristine'. Ellermans should have got their money back if she had just been repainted. Context also matters: where and when photos were taken is lacking all too often; over one third in 'Cargo Ships' and over half in its companion are undated; others have only an estimate. A similar proportion of 'Cargo Ships' do not have locations, although that for the liners is better.

Errors have crept in; *Duchess of Bedford* was intended to become *Empress of India* ('Passenger Liners in Colour', page 20) after war service but George Musk and other authorities record that this never happened because India became independent in 1947. And there is a later edition of his 'Canadian Pacific' than that cited (ibid, page 80), published in the UK by David and Charles. In 'Cargo Ships' the Introduction acknowledges problems of dealing succinctly with ownership but the principles are not applied consistently: *Arabia* was never owned by Cunard ('Cargo Ships', page 20) but on charter: the vessel shown is a different one from that described in the caption.

The Introduction to 'Cargo Ships' opines on differences between cargo liners and tramps, but few tramping companies are represented. Interesting fleets and trades such as Manchester Liners, Bowater, and Hogarths or groundbreaking vessels of Watts, Watts and Co. do not feature. I am disappointed there is no Liberty ship and few wartime standards. The sole SD14 is from outside the timeframe. 'Passenger Liners' is dominated by Cunard, P&O and its antecedents and Union Castle, which account for over half the images.

It is a pity that design and editing detract from the finer pictures. But these books are still to be recommended. In 25 years time will we look favourably on volumes for early purpose-built container ships or vehicle carriers from 1975 to 2000?

Martin Wright

Review follow up

I have read the reviews of two of my recent publications in 'Record' 36. I hope that you will allow me to comment on these reviews, especially as the books were not submitted to you for review.

Firstly, I wish to deal with 'Coasters of the Manchester Ship Canal'. The reviewer is quite correct in noting that the captions say little about the ownership of the ships in the book. Ownership is and always has been a vexed question so it rarely features in any of my books. Do readers really want a meaningless list of company names, many of them leasing companies, for ships that might have passed through the hands of a dozen or more owners during a lifetime of, say, 30 years? Furthermore, the captions do not give dimensions, nor engine details. I know there are readers who are interested in the latter. As a matter of policy, I try to list all previous names of ships in my captions because, in my experience based on feedback, readers often remember seeing a ship under a previous or later name and they can then make a connection between the image on the page and their own observation.

The reviewer is wrong in stating blandly that the 'criteria (sic) for choice (of photographs) has been to show as many locations as possible'. Sadly, he has clearly failed to realise that another criterion was to see the vessels in the context of the weather which, along the Manchester Ship Canal, can be notoriously fickle - to say the least. So, there are photographs in rain, sun, storm and even what he notes as 'flat summer light'. Incidentally, the photograph to which he took particular objection was praised by one reader who had lived in the area for almost two decades and who noted 'that atmospheric photograph perfectly captured so many so-called summer days at Partington.' It is also worth noting that your reviewer picks out the work of three photographers for special mention. Another reviewer selected the work of a different photographer altogether!

I now move on to 'Bristol Channel Shipping Memories'. I am surprised to see that the reviewer feels that the book 'is let down by the quality of its captions'. This is not the opinion of other reviewers. 'Interesting and informative captions' says the 'Ships Monthly' review; 'the photographs are accompanied by well-written explanations of the vessels' histories' comments the

'Telegraph' review. Your reviewer continues, 'The captions are jerkily written, packed with disjointed facts, and too many contain errors or questionable statements that had this reviewer bristling.' Your readers may like to know that all my publications are scrutinised by four readers at the pre-proof stage. Two readers are considered to be experts in maritime knowledge, two know almost nothing of maritime matters but examine grammatical content and literary style. One of the latter is an English graduate. The book, with inevitable alterations, passed the demands of all four readers prior to publication. This is not to say that the book does not contain errors. Show me a book that doesn't!! Even the venerable Ships in Focus 'Record 'series contains them. Presumably that is the reason for the 'Putting the Record straight' articles. Without being too pedantic, even the very reviews which are the subject of this reply contain one grammatical error and one typo. These did not make me bristle, though.

I have left to the end the one sentence in the review which gives me most cause for concern. It reads, 'Clearly the writer has less feel for the ships than his photographer father'. It is one thing to comment on accuracy or photographic content (or even, quality of reproduction or presentation or value for money none deemed worthy of mention in the reviews); it is a different matter altogether to make a personal comment about an author. The comment is as untrue as it is offensive.
BERNARD McCALL, 'Halia', 400 Nore Road, Portishead, Bristol BS20 8EZ

As reviewer I stoutly defend my comments on the two books in question, although no personal offence was meant to Andrew Wiltshire, and I should have said 'the captions do not reflect the feel for ships evidenced by the photographs.' I do not propose to answer Bernard's other points: it is left to readers to make up their minds.

In a separate communication Bernard queries the inclusion of unsolicited reviews in 'Record'. We have a right to publish what we like about any book, so long as it is decent and not libellous, and argue that a review of a book we have paid for is likely to be more objective than one resulting from the largesse of a publisher. However, Bernard has requested that we do not review any more of his works, to which we accede. Roy Fenton

BOSUN'S LOCKER
John Clarkson

Clive Guthrie

Ships in Focus lost a good friend in February, when Clive Guthrie died suddenly whilst awaiting heart surgery. A native of Newcastle-under-Lyme in the Potteries, Clive was by profession an electrical engineer, spending his entire career at Meaford Power Station. By inclination he was an enthusiast for almost all kinds of transport and industrial history. His first love was railways, and he was a strong supporter of a local preserved industrial line, the Foxfield Railway. But in the 1980s he developed a growing interest in shipping, frequently visiting Eastham for photography, and later going further afield on WSS and other trips. He combined his strong feeling for local industrial history and an enthusiasm for ships and other craft by researching in impressive depth the Cheshire shipyard of W.J. Yarwood and its predecessors. He left no stone unturned in pursuing his inquiries into the yard, its personalities and the vessels it built. At the time of his death, and although somewhat slowed by ill health, Clive had almost completed final revisions to his typescript. Ships in Focus are determined to publish his monumental work on Yarwoods, as a tribute to someone who took a genuine interest in our work. Roy and I will miss Clive: it was such a pleasure to break journeys on the M6 for a cup of tea and a chat. Our condolences to his widow, Chris, and to children Jill, Richard and Helen.

Containers: the early years

David Burrrell agrees with my comments that the claims of North Americans to have been in the forefront of development of the container do not stand examination. In terms of their 'inter-modal' capability, the ability to move from one form of transport to another, David reckons containers originated in the 18th century, and were in use by the time of the Liverpool and Manchester Railway. In Victorian times British railways used containers, called lift vans, to move furniture over both roads and railways. In the early 20th century US railroads used them regularly and by 1910 a New York company was sending round the world containers not unlike today's 40-foot units.

Invitation in 'Record' 35

No information has come to light on the reasons for the invitation, but John Woodley has a suggestion for the colours on the flag. During his first trip to sea in 1956 he was told that the colours of his Merchant Navy tie were navy blue for deep water, green for shallow water, white to indicate broken water and red for blood. He speculates that the flag on the invitation has a progression from navy blue for deep water, green for shallow water, light green or grey as broken water, and brown indicating rocks.

Photographs in 'Record' 36

1/36. The consensus is that this ship is the Great Eastern Railway's steamer *Archangel*, ex *St. Petersburg*. Geoffrey Holmes, Tony Smith and Tony Smythe all draw this conclusion, but perhaps the most definite response is from Jerzy Swieszkowski, shipping specialist of the Great Eastern Railway Society, who gives the fullest details of her career. Her raised forecastle is unique amongst railway steamers, and although the Great Eastern's *Stockholm* was designed with a similar arrangement, she was taken over by the Admiralty prior to launch and completed as the seaplane carrier HMS *Pegasus*.

The triple-screw turbine steamer *St Petersburg* was launched in April 1910 by John Brown and Co. Ltd., Clydebank as yard number 394. From entering service in July 1910 to August 1914 she operated on her owner's overnight service from Parkeston Quay to the Hook of Holland. She was then hastily converted to a hospital ship, but made just one cross-Channel voyage as such, in October 1914, before being laid up. She was then converted to a troop transport, and from May 1915 to November 1918 ran from Southampton to Le Havre, Rouen and Cherbourg, being renamed *Archangel* in November 1915. From November 1918 to January 1919 she made ten voyages

Above: *Archangel* wrecked near Aberdeen in May 1941. *[Jerzy Swieszkowski collection]*.
Below: *Empress of China* on a reef in Tokyo Bay in 1911. *[World Ship Society Ltd.]*

between Hull and Rotterdam on behalf of the Great Central Railway before a return to cross-Channel trooping from January to April 1919, during which time she repatriated prisoners-of-war. Because of her being dressed overall, Geoff Holmes speculates that photograph 1/36 shows her on such a voyage, although there is a suggestion that it was taken on Armistice Day, 11th November 1918. In August 1919 after reconditioning she resumed North Sea services for her owners, who in 1923 were to become the London and North Eastern Railway.

In September 1939 *Archangel* again became a troop ship running out of Southampton to France and helped with the evacuation of St. Valery and of Jersey. Following another brief lay up, she began running from Aberdeen to Scapa Flow and Kirkwall in April 1941. During one of these voyages on 17th May 1941 she was bombed by German aircraft off Fraserburgh and suffered three serious hits. Escort HMS *Blankney* took off survivors, but casualties were heavy, comprising 34 of the crew killed and 43 of her military passengers, whilst many more were injured. The *Archangel* was beached north of Aberdeen and quickly broke up. The accompanying photograph of the wreck shows that during the Second World War her hull was black, helping to confirm that photograph 1/36 shows her during the First World War.

2/36. This is one of the three express ships which the Canadian Pacific Railway put into service between Vancouver, Japan and Hong Kong in 1891: *Empress of China*, *Empress of India* and *Empress of Japan*. Of these, *Empress of China* was wrecked in 1912 and, Tony Smythe reckons, never acquired the extra lifeboat abreast the bridge. *Empress of India* had a figurehead of

Queen Victoria, and this and the scrollwork were rather different from those in photograph 2/36 – Robert Langlois kindly provided a copy of an illustration which shows the figureheads of all three. The most likely of the three is therefore *Empress of Japan*, scrapped in 1926 and whose figurehead of a dragon was placed in Stanley Park, Vancouver and is now in that city's maritime museum. Tony Smith endorses this identification, and kindly supplied the accompanying photograph of *Empress of China* ashore on Mera Reef, Tokyo Bay on 21st July 1911. She remained here for over 12 months before being towed away for scrap. Thanks also to Stephen Brophy and John Wilterding junior for their contributions.

3/36. The identity of this Clan Line ship has been definitely established by Archie Munro. She is one of a trio of refrigerator ships dating from 1936, distinguished by an arrangement of 10-ton derricks on the foreside of the foremast and aft side of the main which was not repeated on any subsequent Clans. They were built to handle rolling stock and were designed to allow a railway carriage to be stowed on either side of the boat deck. To handle these the samson post at the aft end of that deck had fittings and stiffening to carry a 30-ton derrick, although all pre-war pictures of these ships show only *Clan Macaulay* actually carried that derrick. Photograph 3/36 clearly shows the 30-ton derrick on the samson post, so can only be *Clan Macaulay*. Archie believes it was taken in Alexandria, Port Said or Piraeus during the period September 1940 to March 1941. Tony Smythe, Tony Smith and A.D. Frost all support the identification as *Clan Macaulay*.

Photographs for identification

1/37. Long-term supporter John B. Hill would like to know more about this paddle steamer, *Aileen*, which may have been photographed on the Tyne.

2/37. It is sometime since we carried a photo of a Blue Funnel ship in *Record* and a first for the old bosun. We know the ship is the *Beagle*, completed in 1892 at Port Glasgow and owned by the Ocean Steam Ship Co. Ltd. What has happened to her - is this the aftermath of a violent storm or cyclone?

3/37. The lower middle picture includes some sort of barge (see enlargement) which is well above river level, packed up on blocks, almost in someone's garden and fitted with what may be a dodger or very primitive bridge. Anyone any ideas on the port or river?

4/37. Where was the bottom photo taken and more importantly what is the ship? She has been fastened back to the land with block and tackle to try to prevent her from rolling over. Fitted with a towing beam she could be a tug but the stairway makes one think more of a tug/tender.